Alexander

AND HIS TIMES

Frédéric Theulé
Art direction by Olivier Laboureur

A Henry Holt Reference Book
Henry Holt and Company
New York

A PICTURE IS WORTH A THOUSAND WORDS

Xun Zi (313-238 B.C.)

聞者不若見之

中耀書荀子語录

Henry Holt and Company, Inc.
Publishers since 1866
115 West 18th Street
New York, New York 10011

Henry Holt ® is a registered trademark
of Henry Holt and Company, Inc.

Published in Canada by Fitzhenry & Whiteside Ltd.,
195 Allstate Parkway, Markham, Ontario L3R 4T8.

Library of Congress Cataloging-in-Publication Data
Theulé, Frédéric.
[Alexandre et Son Temps. English]
Alexander and his times/Frédéric Theulé.
p. cm.
—(W5 (who, what, where, when, and why) series)
Includes bibliographical references and index.
1. Alexander, the Great, 356–323 B.C. 2. Generals—
Greece—Biography. 3. Greece—Kings and rulers—
Biography. 4. Greece—History—Macedonian Expansion,
359–323 B.C. I. Title II. Series.
DF234.T4413   1996   95-40040
938'.07—dc20   CIP
ISBN 0-8050-4657-7

Henry Holt books are available for special
promotions and premiums.
For details contact: Director, Special Markets.

Originally published in France in 1996 by
Editions Mango under the title *Alexandre et Son Temps*.

First published in the United States in 1996 by
Henry Holt and Company, Inc.

First American Edition—1996

Art direction by Olivier Laboureur
Idea and series by Dominique Gaussen
American English translation by Constantin Marinescu
Typesetting by Jay Hyams and Christopher Hyams Hart

Printed in France

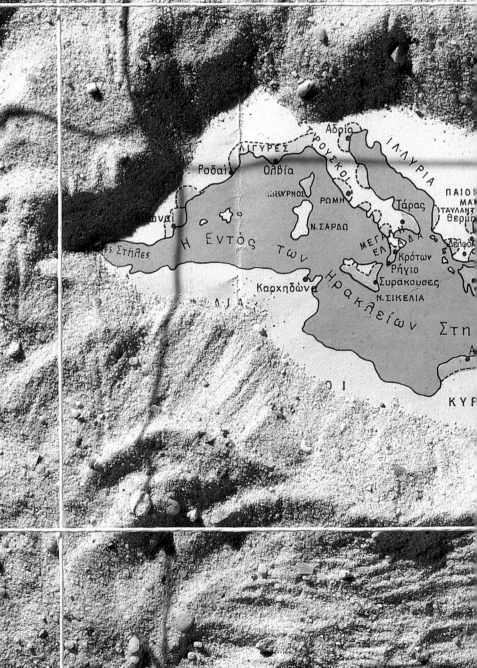

I s the earth shaped like a disk? Do you risk falling off the edge of the earth if you venture too far upon the sea? Does Greece float on water? Between the sixth and the fourth centuries B.C., Greek geographers ask lots of questions and come up with many potential solutions. Among all these hypotheses, the one stating that the earth is round slowly catches on. But the world that the Greeks know is far smaller than ours, stretching from the Strait of Gibraltar to modern Lebanon, and from Austria to Afghanistan. For Greek navigators, the inhabited world has a name: the *oikoumen*. Who lives beyond the Mediterranean coastline? What kind of people would you meet when venturing farther inland? An impetuous voyager, a "globetrotter" before his time, the Greek historian Herodotus (484-420 B.C.) is categorical: except for the Greeks living on

NTO THE WORLD
BE DISCOVERED

Ευξεινος Πόντος

ΠΑΦΛΑΓΟΝΙΑ

ΦΡΥΓΙΑ ΚΑΠΑΔΟΚΙΑ

Αβυδος
ΜΥΔΙΑ ΚΙΛΙΚΙΑ
Εφεσσος ΠΑΜΦΥΛΙΑ
Μιλητος

ΗΤΗ
Ν. ΚΥΠΡΟΣ ΣΥΡΙΑ
θάλασσα
ΦΟΙΝΙΚΙΚΗ
ία
Ναύκρατις

ΙΚΗ

Νειλα

the mainland and those from various cities founded along the Mediterranean, the world is populated only by "barbarians." The main characteristic of these "barbarians" is that they do not speak Greek! (Our word *barbarian* comes from a Greek word meaning "babbler.") This simple distinction is enough to establish a hierarchy among human beings. Herodotus writes (*Histories*): "The Greek stock from the most ancient times has been distinguished from the barbarians for its cleverness and for being free from silly simplemindedness." This idea shows up in the works of the Greek philosopher Aristotle (384-322 B.C.), who repeats the "old" saying: "'Tis meet that Greeks should rule barbarians" (*Politics*). When Alexander comes into the world, the Greeks might know the world's shape, but they still have a lot to learn.

Roman age

Greek age

Egyptian age

6

FROM EGYPT TO GREECE, FROM GREECE TO ROME

*Greek art
2500 B.C.*

From Egypt to Greece and from Greece to Rome; between the fourth millennium B.C. and the birth of Jesus Christ, three great civilizations flourish along the Mediterranean basin and leave their mark on history. One by one they attain military, commercial, and cultural unification, and one by one they rise and fall as if passing on an invisible baton.

At the time of the Egyptian king Ramses II, the Greeks have already started their development. This is the so-called palatial period (2100-1400 B.C.). First in Crete and later at Mycenae in the Peloponnese, large buildings surrounded by villages provide solid testimony of a highly organized society. Archaeologists have discovered such palaces at Knossos, Phaistos, and Mallia on Crete and at Mycenae, Tiryns, and Pylos in the Peloponnese. These palaces are all characterized by large dimensions: central courtyards measuring an average of 3,000 square feet, tall columns and wide pillars, and complex interiors. Astonishingly, in these palaces you can find numerous frescoes that recall the wall paintings of the Egyptians, featuring figures in profile and vivid colors. But who lived there? During Alexander the Great's time people believe that these palaces sheltered fantastic creatures, half-human and half-divine, like the half-man, half-bull Minotaur. Today's historians are more realistic: the inhabitants were king-priests ruling over a hierarchic society dominated by skilled craftsmanship, a society very close to Egypt from the religious point of view. Around 1200 B.C., following many natural disasters and pressured by invaders "coming from the sea," most of the Mycenaean palaces disappear. Much like the Egypt of the pharaohs—then in a state of complete political disarray—Greece experiences troubled times from the twelfth to the eighth centuries B.C. The Greeks abandon all collective life and spread outward in large migratory movements. The result is the foundation of urban centers sprinkled along the Mediterranean, the very cities that will lead the Greek world to its zenith during the fifth century B.C. Little by little Greece takes up the torch bequeathed by Egypt's civilization, which after more than 3,000 years of shining has now been extinguished.

From Egypt to Greece, from Greece to Rome: like the Egyptians, so too will the Greeks attain a high point and then decline. After the rule by the city-states, the conquests of Alexander the Great, and the massive movement of Hellenization that follows, a third great civilization will appear: Rome. Coming to power not long after the time of Alexander, the Romans will assume many cultural aspects of their glorious forebears: commercial control over the entire Mediterranean basin, a legal system very similar to the Athenian model, and a complete transfer of the divine pantheon. A civilization never displaces a preceding one without copying it at least a little.

Greek painting showing Egyptian influence

"While he was saying these words the newborn fell to the ground; there was a flash of lightning, thunder resounded, the earth trembled, and the whole world shook" (Pseudo-Callisthenes, *The Romance of Alexander the Great*). Alexander the Great is born at Pella (Macedonia) in the summer of 356 B.C. The son of King Philip II of Macedonia and Olympias—his fourth wife—the child benefits from a very rigorous education. After spending six or seven years in the royal palace of Aegae together with his cousins, he is entrusted to a teacher named Leonidas. A relative of Olympias, this stern man will give a demanding upbringing to the young prince: physical exercises performed before dawn, a simple diet, lessons learned by heart, and faultless discipline. "Leonidas . . . used to open and search the furniture of his chamber and his wardrobe, to see if his mother had left him anything that was delicate or superfluous" (Plutarch, *Lives of the Noble Grecians and Romans*).

Rigorous and traditional, this education is also well-rounded. Together with other *ephebes* (teenagers) of the

WHEN ALEXANDER THE GREAT WAS STILL VERY SMALL

Macedonian aristocracy, the young Alexander learns gymnastics, music, and poetry. By stressing both physical and spiritual qualities, various tutors of the prince engender in him the mental toughness that will serve him throughout his conquest of the East. From horsemanship to the reading of the *Iliad*, from war to art, nothing is left to chance. To top it all off, Alexander is introduced to philosophy by Greece's most famous philosopher, Aristotle himself. With him, Alexander studies botany, metaphysics, literature, as well as literary and scientific criticism. But despite all this, the son of Philip II remains dedicated to the art of war. Very early on his father wants to introduce him to military campaigns, and so at seventeen Alexander participates in the Macedonian war of repression against the Scythians. By eighteen, he is given command of a squadron of 225 men. And despite his young age he wins the confidence and the respect of the Macedonian elite. It is therefore no surprise that when his father dies—stabbed by a man named Pausanias in 336 B.C.—Alexander is unanimously designated as successor. At this time Alexander has reached the ripe old age of twenty.

CLASSICAL GREECE:

At the beginning of the classical age (fifth century B.C.) the Greek peninsula is studded with a multitude of cities. If you were born at that time, you would not consider yourself a Greek, but rather an Athenian, a Theban, a Spartan, or a Corinthian—and these distinctions are important! Having emerged during the archaic period (eighth-sixth centuries B.C.), these city-states are highly organized with particularly strong political and legal systems. The inhabitants are ruled by laws, and institutions are clearly established, but these developments do not prevent rivalries and differences from forming among cities, as exemplified by Athens and Sparta. Athens is a democratic state, Sparta is military. The social organization.in Athens is based on a system of legal and political equality among the citizens, while in Sparta the state instills an ideal of military virtue and

A MOSAIC OF CITIES

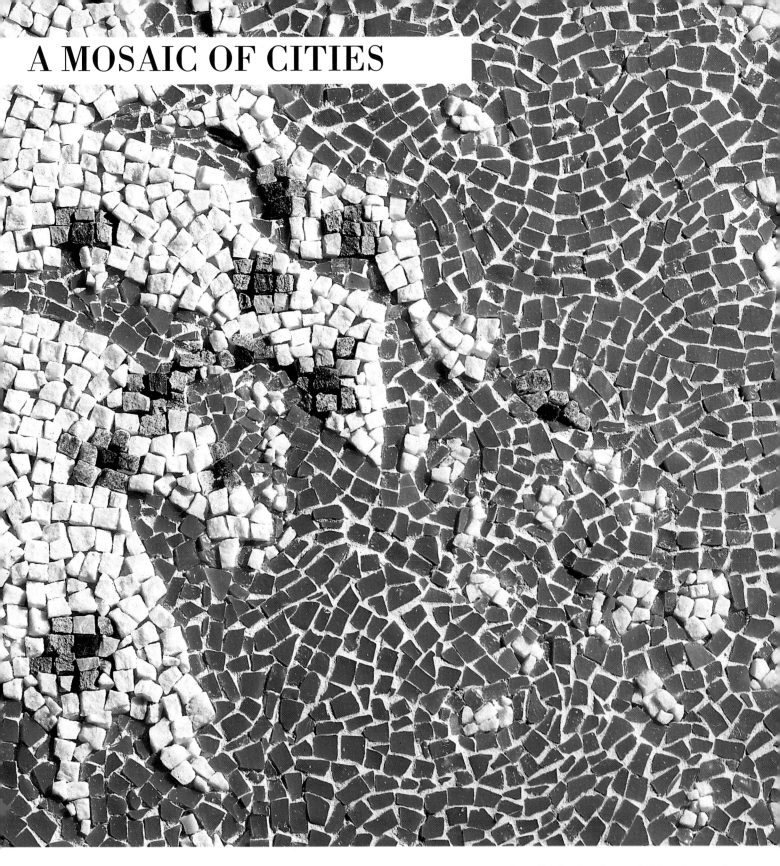

discipline. In Athens *demokratia* (literally, the "authority of people") is slowly developing, with open discussion and debate; Sparta is like an armed camp, ruled in secrecy and with strict military discipline. These two city-states remain antagonistic, with divergent life-styles, for hundreds of years. During the fourth century B.C., however, such diversity among Greek cities slowly vanishes and the mosaic comes together. Philip II, king of Macedon and father of the future Alexander the Great, imposes himself as master of Greece. Athens, and later Thebes, are thoroughly defeated. A "common peace" is concluded at Corinth in 338-337 B.C. This is the famous Corinthian League, which ultimately unites the Greek peninsula by subjecting its main cities to the Macedonian kingdom.

Coin of Philip II

THE GREEK CITY: A LAND WITH A PLAN

With a testimonial by Ricardo Bofill, noted architect

Ricardo Bofill, architect and expert on classicism and modernism

Bold founders of cities and tireless settlers of colonies, the Greeks formulate the first theories of city planning and architecture. Some of the oldest remains preserved today are ruins of the temples of the Athenian tyrant Pisistratus (605-527 B.C.) and Polykrates of Samos, from the fifth century B.C. Because such town plans were so practical, they were copied by other cities. The first city planners, men influenced by reason, logic, and mathematics, are primarily concerned with organizing living space by reconciling the natural shape of the landscape with the symmetry and geometric simplicity of the overall plan. These aspects are found in the Hippodamian city plan, named after Hippodamus of Miletus (fifth century B.C.), the Greek architect famous as the first person to plan cities according to geometric layouts. Also known as the "checkerboard plan," the Hippodamian design was devised to meet practical concerns (the division of land) as well as political needs (social unity) and theoretical aims (the desire for a logical plan). This system is used for the livable area surrounding the *agora* (the city's marketplace, used for assemblies) and the *acropolis* (the elevated area of the city with its fortified citadel and buildings devoted to religious worship), thus per-

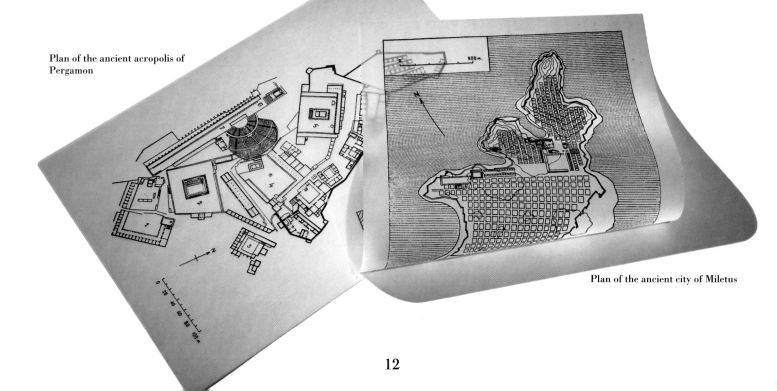

Plan of the ancient acropolis of Pergamon

Plan of the ancient city of Miletus

fectly satisfying the needs of the population.

The layout's simplicity allows you to cross the city without losing your way, but at the same time makes it easy to defend the city from any undesired "visitors"

The temple of Athena Nike on the acropolis of Athens

eager to make it their own. Best known for his work in Piraeus (the port just south of Athens), Hippodamus inspired many city plans. From Olynthus to Alexandria, not to mention a large number of American cities today, the checkerboard plan has been applied over continents and centuries. Were the Greeks truly masters of thinking about actual city planning and architecture? Yes, if you're willing to take the word of contemporary architects like Ricardo Bofill. In fact, instead of denying the influence of the Greek town-planners, Bofill acknowledges them as a source of inspiration for his own work: "The conception of the town conveyed by western civilization goes back to antiquity (Hippodamus of

Port Marianne, Monpellier, France

Wacker Drive, Chicago

The theater of Abraxas,
Marne-la-Vallée, France

Miletus in Greece, and afterward the architects of Roman cities)," Bofill writes in *Taller de Arquitectura*, a book coauthored by Annabelle d'Huart. The same ideas are echoed again: "Codified by Vitruvius, revised

Temples from the Lac de Saint-Quentin-en-Yvelines, France

by the architects of the Renaissance . . . [the principles of classic architecture] have crossed not only geographical frontiers but also centuries" (Ricardo Bofill and Jean-Louis André, *Èspaces d'une vie*). The fundamental Greek principles—emphasizing symmetry, the challenge of social integration, the respect for a certain order—are all found in Bofill's work. He concludes in his book *Taller de Arquitectura*: "It is a pity that during the centuries these simple shapes have been concealed by decoration and ornamentation... It is one of the ambitions of *Taller* to bring to light again the [classical] archetype in its entire whole sobriety." One couldn't dream of a greater homage to Greek city planning.

SLAVES, RESIDENT
PORTRAIT OF A THREE-

Antiquity doesn't rhyme with equality—contrary to the popular notion, not all Greek people are free. Based on an economic and military aristocracy, the society of Alexander the Great shows deep inequalities between three classes of people: citizens, resident aliens, and slaves.

CITIZENS

The most important characteristics of this minority group (since all women are excluded) are owning land and exercising political rights. "A citizen, according to the absolute meaning of the word, cannot better be defined than by participation in the dispensation of justice and the magistracy," affirms the philosopher Aristotle (*Politics*), the contemporary and teacher of Alexander. In most Greek cities citizenship is the result of a strict selection. In Sparta, for example, citizenship is granted by birth as well as a double affirmation: one by your father and another by the assembly of the Ancients of the Tribe. If the latter opposes the affirmation, the newborn is drowned. Sparta is no place for the weak of heart!

RESIDENT ALIENS

This intermediate group is composed of foreigners passing through the city. If these men remain in the city after a certain time (for instance, one month in Athens) they must register as resident aliens. Then they pay a small tax acquiring the right to participate in certain festivals, and thereby the possibility to integrate in mainstream society. Represented in court by a patron (the *prostates*) and compelled according to their wealth to the same financial obligations as citizens (donations, war taxes), the resident aliens can acquire citizenship, but they can also become slaves. Their daily occupations include economic or military activity—artisans, merchants, bankers, oarsmen in the navy, and so on. And it just so happens that sometimes certain resident aliens are richer than the citizens!

SLAVES

"When one needs to clarify an obscure point concerning an event at which both slaves and free men were present, you should not rely upon the testimony of free men, but rather put the slaves to torture" (*On the inheritance of Ciron*). In the fourth century B.C., the orator Isocrates discussed the implicit hierarchy that exists between different human beings. Deprived of family, possessions, and freedom, slaves don't have any rights, and their daily life is regulated by their master. The master has complete control of his slaves; he can even allow or deny them a love life! In fact, the slave is seen as only a piece of property, an inanimate object. This doesn't prevent slaves from benefiting from certain legal protections, particularly in Athens, where it is forbidden for anybody to mistreat them. But set your mind at ease—slaves could be freed, being granted freedom in a will or by buying their freedom. Two outstanding examples are Pasion and Phormion, liberated slaves who become bankers and later citizens during the reign of Alexander the Great. So even during the days of Alexander, you really can make your way up the social ladder.

ALIENS, CITIZENS:
FACED SOCIETY

YOU COULD TELL BY HIS FOREHEAD THAT ALEXANDER WAS BOUND FOR SUCCESS

During the time of the Greeks a method of psychological analysis based on close observation of the human face is created. The name of this new "science" is physiognomy.

What can we tell about the nature of Alexander the Great using this particular mode of analysis? Based on the idealized portrait of the Macedonian conqueror when he was only a teenager (the portrait on the page opposite) we can establish certain characteristics. The wide forehead, deep-set eyes, high and protruding cheekbones suggest that the young Macedonian is intelligent, an aesthete (lover of the arts), and is full of integrity, all while remaining docile and obedient. Aestheticism, integrity, intelligence: we find these same characteristics in the adult Alexander, as in the portrait sculpted by Lysippus, a contemporary of Alexander (see below right). Here the vanquisher of Darius seems more assertive, accomplished, and complex. No more docility here: the valiant nose (thought to indicate a desire for challenges and activity), the big vertical wrinkles crossing the cheeks (emotional suffering), the square and projecting chin (strategical genius and the need to know himself) testify to a more complex psychology. At once a master of himself but also capable of sudden wrath, ambitious but also altruistic, Alexander seems to have evolved from his early days. A significant fact: this analysis is corroborated by numerous chroniclers and historians. Will study of physiognomy help us learn more about history? Maybe, but you'll probably have a hard time convincing the folks at Harvard.

Large, high forehead and rounded temples:
an open mind, curiosity, encyclopedic memory

Fleshy eyelids:
intuition, delicacy, feminine demeanor

Deep-set eyes:
capacity for thought, artistic sensibility

Broad base of the nose:
spiritual sensibility

High cheekbones: sense of aesthetics, generosity, need for ideals and purity

Small, fleshy mouth with distinctive contours (also childish or feminine):
sensitivity and need of tenderness

Small, but jutting chin:
limited physical strength but ability for rapid actions

In Alexander's Greece, there is no single church or faith and instead religious life is characterized by great variety. First of all, there is a crowd of minor divinities (like minor-league gods): nymphs, naiads, river gods, demons—the Greeks see the divine everywhere! In addition to these minor Gods, the Greeks also worship demigods (half-human, half-god), the most famous of whom is Herakles (known to the Romans as Hercules), who greatly inspires Alexander. Then there is a multitude of religious practices, from simple offerings and libations to communal rituals (some like banquets) at temples; the means for petitioning the gods are certainly not lacking. Finally there is a variety of cults: local faiths differ greatly, with different gods and goddesses popular in different cities and regions. While there may not be

GET YOUR GREEK GODS

ZEUS	**POSEIDON**	**DEMETER**	**PLUTO/HADES**	**DIONYSUS**	**ATHENA**
Son of Cronos and Rhea. *Lord of the sky and most powerful of the gods; source of life and fertility.* *Symbols: thunderbolt, globe, eagle, throne, serpent, scepter, oak tree.*	*Son of Cronos and Rhea and brother of Zeus.* *God of the sea (especially when storming), associated with fertility—as god of the water he fertilized the earth; known as Earth-shaker (earthquakes are his doing) Symbols: trident, fish, horse, dolphin.*	*Daughter of Cronos and Rhea.* *Goddess of the fertility of the earth (which engenders civilized life); the one who brings human beings into the mysteries of fertilization and of the afterlife. Symbols: wheat spike, pig.*	*Son of Cronos and Rhea and brother of Zeus.* *God of the underworld and ruler of the dead; master of the wealth beneath the earth. Symbols: three-headed dog Cerberus, cornucopia, underground silos.*	*Son of Zeus and Semele, a mortal woman.* *God of fertility and wine, of mystic ecstasy and divine inspiration. Symbols: grapes, vine, wine, gigantic phallus.*	*Born of Zeus alone.* *Goddess of the city, protector of civilized life, of handicrafts, agriculture, and the health of children and adolescents. The embodiment of wisdom; in time of war she is the goddess of intelligence and cunning. Symbols: owl, spear, serpent, aegis (her shield), olive tree.*

much agreement on religious practices, all the Greeks know and recognize the basic *pantheon* (from a Greek word meaning "all the gods") composed of twelve great gods (the major leaguers) who live on Mount Olympus and are thus known as Olympians. The twelve Olympians form a divine family. For example, Ares, famous as the god of war, is the son of Zeus and Hera, and Zeus's sister Hestia is the goddess of the hearth and home. Each god has his or her sphere of power. If your ship is caught in a storm, you'll probably pray to Poseidon for help (and offer him a hefty sacrifice when you get back on dry land). If you're lost in the woods, Hermes may fly by to show you the path. And if you're sick, Apollo will know the cure. While you might be able to tell them apart without a scorecard, having one handy probably wouldn't hurt.

SCORECARD HERE!

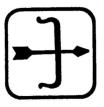     

ARTEMIS	APHRODITE	APOLLO	HEPHAESTUS	HERMES	HERA
Daughter of Zeus and Leto and Apollo's twin sister. Protector of all wild animals, goddess of the hunt, of trees and rivers, of female chastity and independence from male constraints. Symbols: bow, deer, cypress, walnut tree, breasts.	Daughter of Zeus and Dione and wife of Hephaestus. Goddess of fecundity (including sexual union, procreation, and the education of children), love (passion and sentiment), and beauty. Symbols: dove, apple, myrtle tree, shells.	Son of Zeus and Leto and twin brother of Artemis. God of light and truth, music and medicine; the direct link between gods and humans, guiding humans to know divine will and the truth; the far-shooting archer god. Symbols: musical instruments, chariot, bow, laurel, obelisk, pillar, deer, swan, dolphin.	Son of Zeus and Hera (or just Hera alone) and husband of Aphrodite. The god of fire, armor maker and blacksmith of the gods with his forge under the volcano Mount Etna. The only ugly god (also lame). Symbols: fire, forge.	Son of Zeus and Maia. Messenger of the gods, protector of travelers and merchants; guide of the dead to the underworld; known as the Master Thief and the shrewdest and most cunning of the gods. Symbols: winged-sandals, petasus (low, broad hat, also with wings), caduceus (his rod, topped by wings and entwined by two serpents—later the emblem of the medical profession).	Daughter of Cronos and wife (and also sister) of Zeus. Protector of marriage and married women, of feminine life, of childbirth, of a city's high places (for example, the palaces). Symbols: peacock, cow, baths, flowers, lily, moon.

THE GREEKS AND THE PERSIANS:

Greeks against Persians, Persians against Greeks—during the fifth century B.C. a great antagonism divides the Easterners (the Persians) from the Westerners (the Greeks). The seeds of the conflict lie in the conquest by Persian king Cyrus I (died 529 B.C.) of a huge kingdom encompassing modern Iran and the west coasts of Asia Minor, a region in which there are many Greek colonies. Cyrus's successors consolidate this empire and then expand into Egypt, leading the Persians on a collision course with the Greeks, who want to retain their way of life and their freedom. Faced with the gradually strengthening

Persian influence, the Greek colonies on the Asian shores of the Aegean Sea form a league and decide to rebel. The revolt ignites suddenly at the beginning of the fifth century B.C. and eventually involves Byzantium and the cities of Caria and Cyprus. And surprisingly enough, during the first clash in the conflict the Greeks of Asia—supported by several mainland cities, including Athens—succeed in destroying Sardis, one of the Persian capitals. The trauma of this defeat is enormous to the Persians, making them eager for revenge. In 490 they organize a punitive expedition against the cities of the Greek peninsula that helped the

WHY CAN'T THEY JUST GET ALONG?

insurgents. Their plan is to add Greece to their enormous empire. This is the beginning of the Persian Wars. The decisive battle takes place on the plain of Marathon, where the Athenian hoplites, or infantrymen, win a great victory against the Persians. Think this is enough to discourage the courageous Persians? Far from it! In 481, Xerxes, the successor of Darius, returns to the attack with 350,000 men and a fleet of 750 ships. This time, the Greeks are forced to yield to the Persians. In the pass at Thermopylae, the Spartans cannot halt the advance of the Persians, who take the city of Athens, completely destroying it and its vener-

ated sanctuaries. Now, it's the Greeks' turn to know the agony of defeat. Plataea (479), Mycale (479), Eurymedon (468)—the battles rage on. Trapped in an unending cycle, the Persians and Greeks mount punitive expeditions and vengeful counteroffensives. The leaders on both sides have a single goal in mind: to avenge their ancestors slaughtered in battle by the enemy. Alexander the Great will not escape this vicious cycle and follows in the footsteps of his father, Philip II of Macedon (382-336 B.C.): during a period of two years the great conqueror consolidates his empire and then, in 334, he turns his attention to the Persian East.

Stories and tales swirl around Alexander, some the reflections of historical reality, some the concoctions of overzealous biographers. The 🅦 staff investigated four episodes from the life of the Macedonian conqueror: Bucephalus, the Gordian knot, Alexander's divine birth, and the Amazons. Each episode is

THE DIVINE ANCESTRY OF ALEXANDER

"His father, Philip . . . fell in love with Olympias and married her. **The night before the consummation of their marriage, she dreamed that a thunderbolt fell upon her body, which kindled a great fire, whose divided flames dispersed themselves all about, and then were extinguished.** *And Philip, some time after he was married, dreamt that he sealed up his wife's body with a seal, whose impression, as he fancied, was the figure of a lion. . . .* Once, moreover, a serpent was found lying by Olympias as she slept, *which more than anything else, it is said, abated Philip's passion for her; and whether he feared her as an enchantress, or thought she had commerce with some god, and so looked on himself as excluded, he was ever after less fond of her"* (Plutarch, Lives of the Noble Grecians and Romans).

THE AMAZONS

"When Alexander returned to Hyrcania, *there came to him the queen of the Amazons named Thalestris, who ruled all the country between the rivers Phasis and Thermodon. She was remarkable for beauty and for bodily strength, and was admired by her countrywomen for bravery. She had left the bulk of her army on the frontier of Hyrcania and had arrived with an escort of three hundred Amazons in full armor. The king marveled at the unexpected arrival and the dignity of the women. When he asked Thalestris why she had come,* **she replied that it was for the purpose of getting a child. He had shown himself the greatest of all men in his achievements, and she was superior to all women in strength and courage, so that presumably the offspring of such outstanding parents would surpass all other mortals in excellence.** *At this the king was delighted and granted her request and consorted with her for thirteen days, after which he honored her with fine gifts and sent her home"* (Diodorus Siculus, Universal History).

FICTION?

a mixture of facts, uncertainties, and lies. Here below we present in regular type the historical events, those we know to have actually occurred; in *italic* type are those parts of each story that may have drifted from reality; and in **bold** type are the out-and-out falsehoods. Read carefully!

BUCEPHALUS

"Philonicus the Thessalian brought the horse Bucephalus to Philip, offering to sell him for thirteen talents; but when they went into the field to try him, they found him so very vicious and unmanageable that he reared up when they endeavored to mount him and would not so much as endure the voice of any of Philip's attendants. *Upon which, as they were leading him away as wholly useless and untractable, Alexander, who stood by, said, 'What an excellent horse do they lose for want of address and boldness to manage him!' . . . He securely mounted him, and when he was seated, by little and little he drew in the bridle and curbed him without either striking or spurring him. Presently, when he found him free from all rebelliousness, and only impatient for the course, he let him go at full speed, inciting him now with a commanding voice, and urging him also with his heel. Philip and his friends looked on at first in silence and anxiety for the result,* **till seeing him turn at the end of his career, and come back rejoicing and triumphing for what he had performed, they all burst out into acclamations of applause; and his father shedding tears, it is said, for joy, kissed him as he came down from his horse,** *and in his transport said, 'O my son, look thee out a kingdom equal to and worthy of thyself, for Macedonia is too little for thee'*" (Plutarch, Lives).

THE GORDIAN KNOT

"He subdued the Pisidians who made head against him, and conquered the Phrygians, at whose chief city, Gordium, *which is said to be the seat of the ancient Midas, he saw the famous chariot fastened with cords made of the rind of the cornel-tree, which whosoever should untie, the inhabitants had a tradition, that for him was reserved the empire of the world. Most authors tell the story that Alexander finding himself unable to untie the knot, the ends of which were secretly twisted round and folded up within it, cut it asunder with his sword.* **But Aristobulus tells us it was easy for him to undo it, by only pulling the pin out of the pole, to which the yoke was tied, and afterward drawing off the yoke itself from below**" (Plutarch, Lives).

THE ORIGINAL AND THE CARL LEWIS

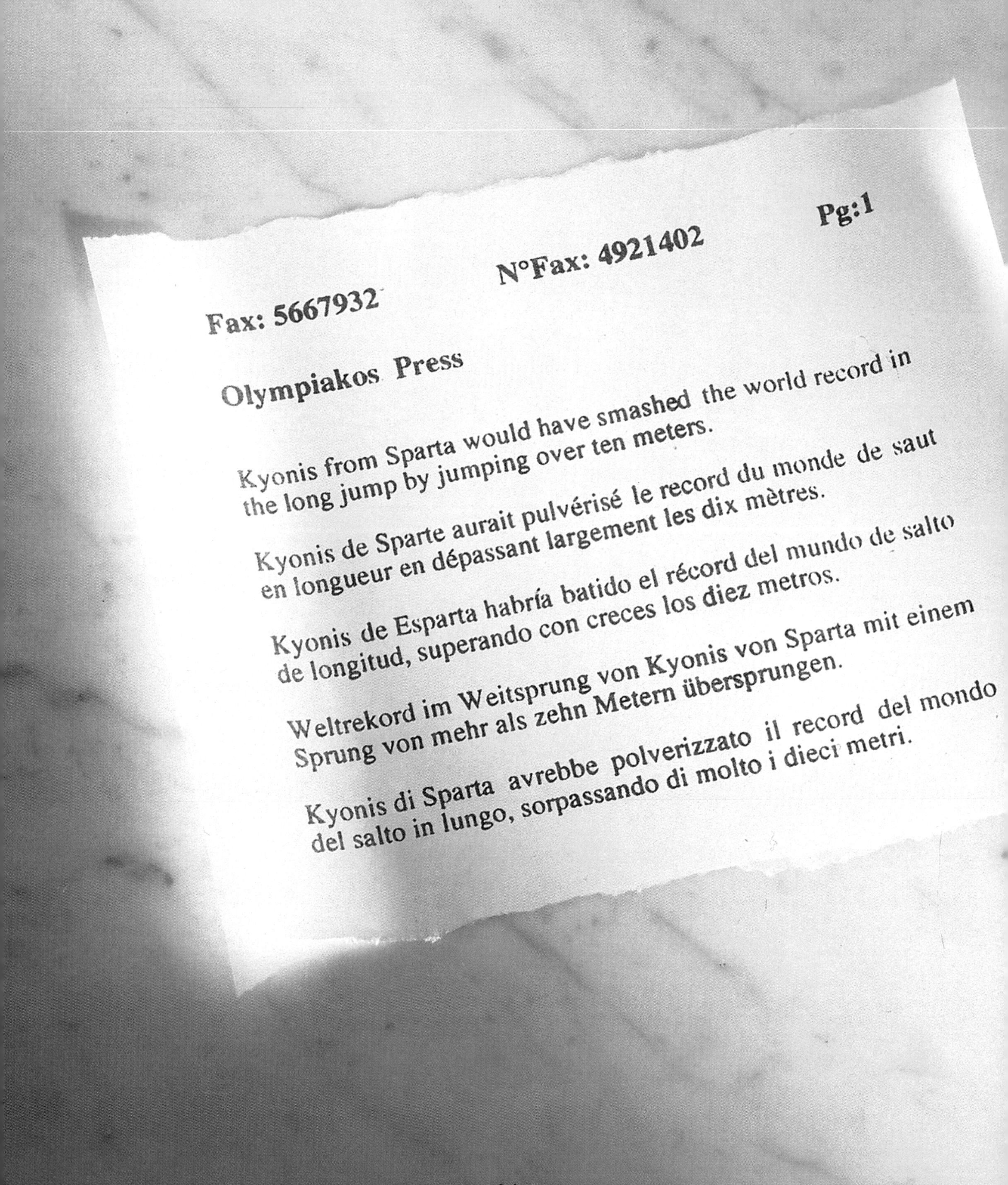

Fax: 5667932 N°Fax: 4921402 Pg:1

Olympiakos Press

Kyonis from Sparta would have smashed the world record in the long jump by jumping over ten meters.

Kyonis de Sparte aurait pulvérisé le record du monde de saut en longueur en dépassant largement les dix mètres.

Kyonis de Esparta habría batido el récord del mundo de salto de longitud, superando con creces los diez metros.

Weltrekord im Weitsprung von Kyonis von Sparta mit einem Sprung von mehr als zehn Metern übersprungen.

Kyonis di Sparta avrebbe polverizzato il record del mondo del salto in lungo, sorpassando di molto i dieci metri.

OLYMPIC GAMES OF YESTERYEAR!

"Soon after came the day of the competition. Nine charioteers were on the track, among them four sons of kings: Nikolaos, Xanthias the Boetian, Kimon of Corinth, and Alexander himself . . . The competitors mounted their chariots and advanced to the starting point" (Pseudo-Callisthenes, *The Romance of Alexander the Great*). Like most Greek teenagers, the young Alexander participates in numerous athletic trials and contests. Instruments by which cities peacefully assert their identity, these competitions allow each generation to define itself, and they also stimulate the sense of healthy competition among the citizens. By far the best and most famous of these games are those held at Olympia (western Peloponnesus): the Olympic Games.

First held in 776 B.C., the Olympic Games take place every four years in the summer. For a period of six days athletes from all the cities of the Greek world, whether from the mainland or elsewhere on the Mediterranean sea, come together to compete. The Olympic flame shines brightly, accompanying the athletes, all of whom

are male. For the entire time of the competitions the Greeks observe a sacred truce during which all military operations are forbidden. What kind of games are played? Unlike the Olympic Games that we know, the events can be counted on the fingers of your two hands. There are exactly ten: four races, an equestrian race, three contests of fighting (wrestling, boxing, and the *pancratium*, an event that combines boxing and wrestling), the pentathlon (combining the long jump, wrestling, and the discus, the javelin, and the race), and finally the chariot race, the most prestigious of all events. Curious about their uniforms? The Greeks have no need for them, since they compete in the nude (women can neither participate in nor watch the Olympic Games, but they hold games of their own).

Do the Greeks have a hall of fame and record books? It is difficult to tell, since few records have survived, partly because the Greeks show little interest in writing them down. We do know, however, that Coroebus won the foot race in 776, and in the eighth century B.C. Kyonis of Sparta is said to have exceeded 32 feet (over 10 meters) in the long jump! That record is difficult to believe given our own Olympic records.

The winners of all events receive special honors. Besides wearing olive wreathes that are consecrated in the temple of Zeus, they are given valuable gifts and privileges by their proud native cities.

The Athenians sometimes go so far as to erect a statue of the winner in the agora, an honor no doubt befitting someone like Carl Lewis, although he has yet to match Kyonis of Sparta in the long jump.

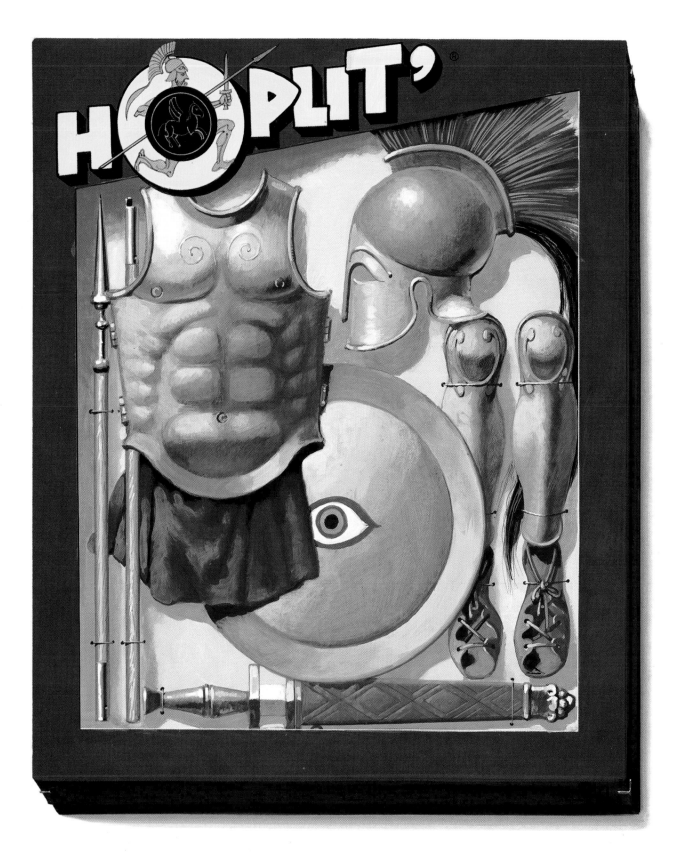

IN PANOPLIES! (WHAT'S A PANOPLY?)

It might seem hard to believe, but the Greek hoplites achieve their spectacular conquests between 334 and 323 B.C. dressed in *panoplia* (a Greek word meaning "full armor"). A primary element of Alexander's army, the panoply is established during the Greek military reforms of the seventh century B.C. It consists of leather sandals, a wooden spear (more than ten feet long), a short sword made of iron, a helmet (round and made of metal), a breastplate (made of metal or layers of hides), greaves, or leg guards, and a round metal shield with a double handle. And guess what—the purchase of all this heavy equipment is the responsibility of the soldier. But "investing" in a cheap *panoplia* is not a good idea: you run the risk of paying the ultimate price on the battlefield! Alexander the Great's soldiers are not all armed in the same way. Cavalry, infantry, mercenaries (hired soldiers)—each unit has its own distinctive equipment. The Agrianians (natives of modern Bulgaria) are equipped with two or three javelins, while cavalry-

men usually carry a curved sword called a *kopis*. The mercenaries are lightly armed (either with a bow or a sling), and for good reason: they're generally used for scouting purposes or for pursuing the enemy.

ALEXANDER'S SECRET

The "trump card" of Alexander's army is undoubtedly the formation called the *phalanx*, a word meaning literally "wooden beam." Between 334 and 323 B.C., the Macedonian phalanx becomes famous on distant battlefields, defeating the Persian and Indian armies one after the other. A formidable weapon of war, the phalanx is composed of

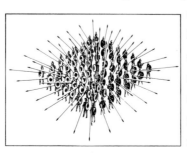

hoplites carrying round shields that cover their left shoulders and slender spears about thirteen feet long (the famous *sarissa*). The men stand in solid ranks with their shields overlapping and their spears thrust forward (the spears are so long that even those carried by the men in the back rows stick out a long way in front). Like a modern-day tank, this bristly

WEAPON: A HEDGEHOG!

formation rolls over enemy units. Each phalanx is led by a *strategus*, the equivalent of our general, who directs his men almost like an orchestra conductor. And this really pays off on the battlefield. Deployed in a straight, slanted, or crescent line, the phalanx can swing around as a solid mass to face an enemy. Because of its bristly appearance, the phalanx has often been compared to an "iron hedgehog." Originally composed of soldiers from a small class of

Macedonians (the *pezetairoi*, primarily free peasants), the phalanx is an elite body. Not everyone can join. Indeed, during a major part of the Eastern conquest only Macedonians have the right to fight in the phalanx. They are driven by a powerful sense of duty as well as by an unfailing devotion to Alexander the Great. A genuine national militia, these soldiers are in many ways the guardians of the Macedonian spirit.

THREE BENCHES OF OARSMEN,

"Alexander took from the treasury of the Macedonians seventy talents of coined gold. He ordered the building of triremes as well as galleys and journeyed from Macedonia through the Thermodon River to Thrace lying to the north. . . then to Sicily where he defeated some elements that were in revolt there before continuing toward the land of Italy. . . . From there Alexander embarked again, crossed the Mediterranean, and arrived in Africa" (Pseudo-Callisthenes, *The Romance of Alexander the Great*). It's thanks to his navy, of course, that Alexander is able to carry

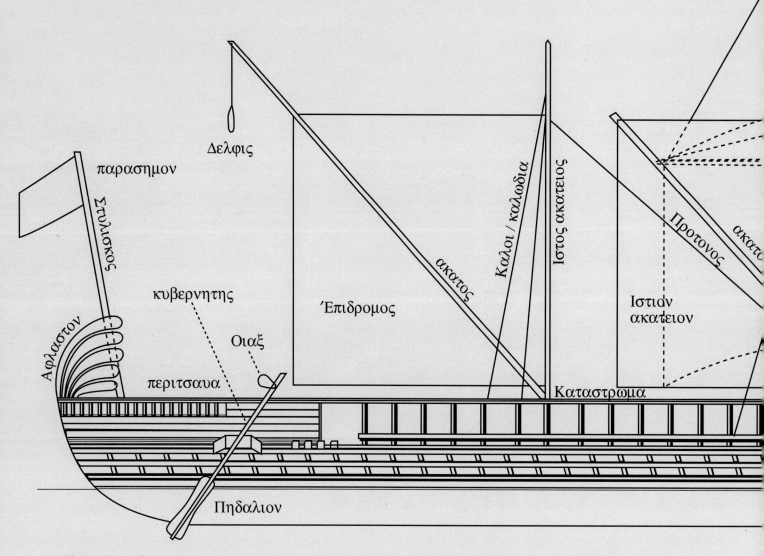

Alexander relies on many types of ship, including *penteres* (five rows of oarsmen), *tetreres* (four rows of oarsmen), and *hemiolia* (often used by pirates). All in all, the navy's fleet makes use of 28 kinds of ship. The most famous among these are the Athenian triremes, Greek warships with three banks of 200 oarsmen and a weight of up to 80 tons. With their triple rows of oars and square sails, these ships are famous throughout the Mediterranean for being extremely maneuverable and fast, with a top speed of up to nine nautical miles an hour. The oars move in unison, with a maximum frequency of 18 beats per minute, regulated by the rhythm of a musical instrument, usually a gong or drum. The triremes' weaponry includes a bronze spike with protruding nails that can be attached to the prow in order to ram and sink enemy ships. Other innovations include naval artillery, which makes its first appearance at this time, with the installation of large catapults and smaller swiveling catapults on the ship's

AND NOT A SINGLE COMPLAINT!

out his conquests between 334 and 323 B.C. The Greeks make their advances across seas, rivers, and small bodies of water using a wide variety of boats. In the spring of 334, there are no fewer than 180 warships (182 to be precise, if we believe the Roman historian Justin), employing nearly as many people as the land army. And this only increases over time: in 325, the expeditionary force that goes down the Indus River numbers 1,800 ships. Warships, transports, pirate ships, attack and fishing vessels—the navy needs all kinds, not just the purely military. The leader of the navy is the admiral Nearchus, a man descended from an illustrious family of Cretan sailors; he has Alexander's full confidence.

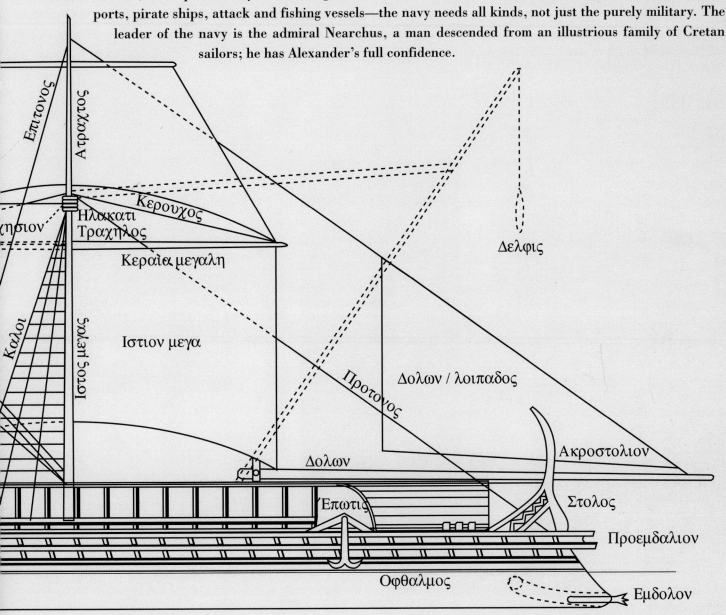

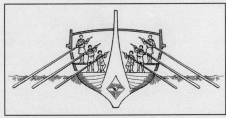

bridge. You can imagine the terror created by these two "novelties," the shock of a ship coming at you at 10 knots, the crash of the hulls, the devastating hole in your vessel, the water rushing to create an instant shipwreck. Life aboard ship is tough. Discipline is more rigorous than on land, and the officers are merciless to the oarsmen. Even so, there is fierce competition to row since only citizens (and occasionally resident aliens) are allowed the "privilege" of manning the long oars; slaves would never be allowed this honor! These select individuals undergo systematic training, with plenty of exercise and simulated maneuvers every day. Three benches of oarsmen. and no man grumbles: can you believe it?

TO CHANGE
THE COURSE OF HISTORY,
ALEXANDER THINKS NOTHING
OF CHANGING GEOGRAPHY

Gaza, Aornos, Massaga—between 334 and 326, Alexander the Great conducts a total of fifteen sieges, but of these the most difficult by far is that of the city of Tyre (in modern Lebanon).

Tyre proves a stubborn city. When the Macedonian conqueror arrives in February 332, the inhabitants of this Phoenician island refuse him access to the sanctuary of Melqart-Herakles, whom Alexander considers to be an ancestor. Deeply offended by the decision of the Tyrian aristocracy and priests, and fresh from his victory at Issus, Alexander does not hesitate: the fortified island will be taken by force!

For many months Alexander's engineers labor away to build a connection between the island and the mainland. Under their command thousands of local workers construct in deep water a giant mole, a wall more than 2,000 feet long and 200 wide. The work pro-gresses slowly since it is carried out under constant fire from enemy archers. While the mole is being built, siege engines are brought to play. These fireproof wooden towers armed with catapults do not impress the besieged Tyrians, and the battle continues. Will Tyre ever be subjugated? Well, if a siege doesn't work, then Alexander will subdue it by sea! After seven months of endless onslaught, in August 332, triremes attack from the north and south. This is the decisive engagement, and it finally destroys the powerful Phoenician tradesmen, allies of the Persian leader Darius. Alexander can rejoice: not only does he control the eastern Mediterranean, but he has succeeded in forever transforming Tyre[1] from an island into a peninsula.

1. Today Tyre is known as Sur, and the mole Alexander built has grown into a large causeway.

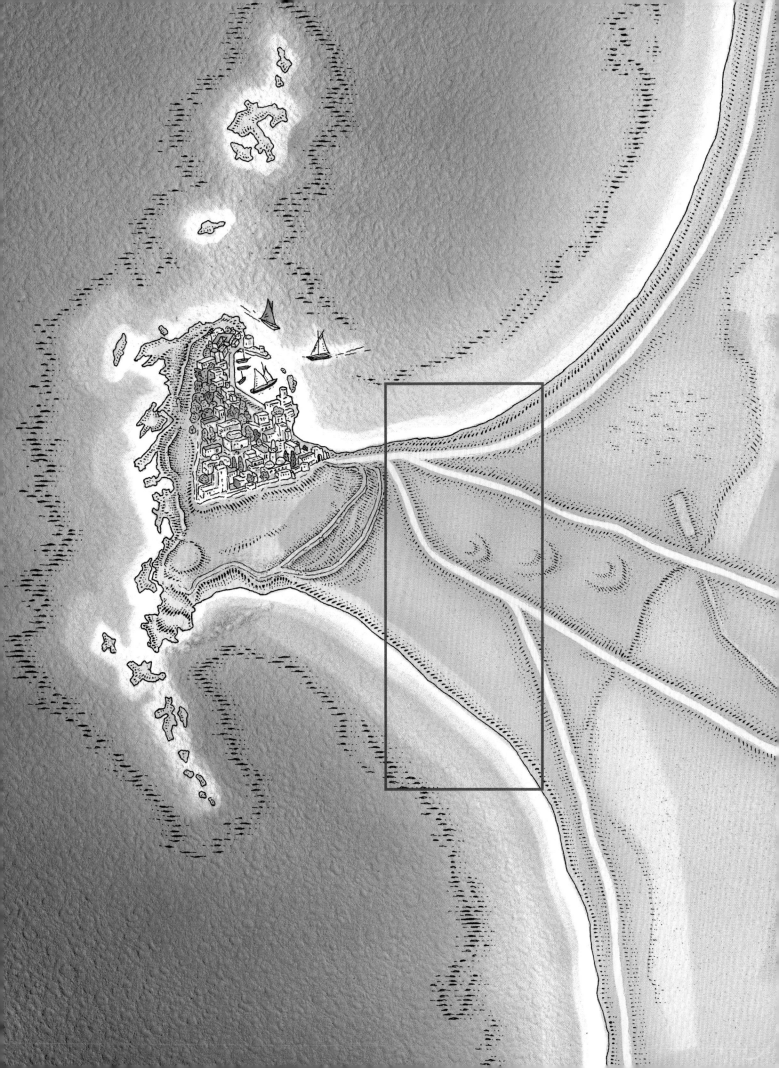

Alexander the Great did not invent artillery, but without doubt it is under his stimulus that it develops rapidly during the fourth century B.C. From the siege of Tyre (332) to those of Avarana (330) and Gaza (332-331) and those carried out in modern Pakistan (326), the Greek armies rely on massive amounts of artillery to besiege cities. Thanks to the discoveries of mechanics, engineers, and technicians, these heavy weapons bring decisive support to the beleaguered Macedonians, who hardly complain about the weight of lugging them around. An outstanding example is Leninabad (in today's Tadzhikistan) in the neighborhood of the Syr Darya River in September 329. Facing the fearsome Scythian cavalry, Alexander commands his engineers to mount the ballistae. Stable and powerful, these weapons, similar to huge crossbows, soon spread terror among the barbarians. Shields, helmets, armor, everything is powerless against these arrows, which are up to three feet

Since the Middle Ages artists have made representatio

long—and that's without mentioning the damage they cause when set on fire before being launched.

Other weapons with equally devastating effects are the *oxybelos* (catapults) and *lithobolos* (stone-hurling machines). Used especially during Alexander's numerous sieges, these

NOT BE TAKEN LIGHTLY

f the siege engines descibed in the chronicles of Alexander.

heavy weapons are the towers. These can be taken apart and reassembled in different forms. Made of wood and metal they reach heights of 60 feet. Each floor has sharpshooters, ballistae, and battering rams. Let's listen to the description of one of these towers told by Diodorus Siculus (*Universal History*): "The whole body was movable and supported by eight solid wheels of colossal dimensions . . . The floors facing the enemy had windows provided with shutters for protection . . . which were covered with skins and padded with wool in order to absorb the blows of the stones. Each floor had two stairways, one to bring up the material and the other one to go down, so that all the servicing was done without disorder. And 3,400 people, chosen for their strength, were in charge of moving the machine, all of them pushing at the same time, some from the interior, others from behind and the sides." Now that's teamwork!

mechanisms can throw 175-pound stone blocks over the walls of besieged fortifications. They have an impressive maximum range of 500 feet. You can easily imagine the gruesome damage made by these massive weapons, the howitzers of their day. The last of the

MAY 334: GRANICUS

This first battle between the armies of Alexander and the Persians takes place near a small river in Phrygia Minor (today in modern Turkey): the Granicus. Quickly joined, the battle is confused, with arrows and stone projectiles raining down on the combatants, and the fighting furious. Easily recognizable by the two white plumes of his helmet, Alexander is soon surrounded by Persians, repeatedly struck, and even thrown to the ground. He is saved only by the timely intervention of one of his most loyal generals, "Black" Cleitus. Just at that moment, the long spears of the Greeks bring about a miracle. Like a steamroller, the Macedonian phalanx pushes back the Persian cavalry and its allies from Asia Minor. Gaining the upperhand, Alexander's forces rout the enemy, and merciless slaughter ensues. Writing four centuries later, Plutarch mentions that after the battle Alexander sent home to Athens hundreds of enemy shields upon which he had inscribed: "Alexander, the son of Philip, and the Grecians . . . won these from the barbarians who inhabit Asia" (Lives).

OCTOBER 331: GAUGAMELA

Exactly two years after Issus, Alexander and Darius face off once again. In the heart of today's Iraq, the trumpets sound anew the attack. Alexander's front line takes its place: the Macedonian phalanx is in the center, the allied armies form a square on the sides, the cavalry is the corner so that it cannot be attacked from the rear. Alexander orders his soldiers: "Aim at the face!" An immense fight follows. The Greeks are terrified as they come to face with chariots bearing scythes and also elephants, animals that—or so the Greeks have been told—can run faster than horses and can withstand the point of a sarissa. Trampled and impaled by the Persian onslaught, Alexander suffers serious losses, but "of the Persian dead were counted some three hundred thousand," according to the Greek historian Arrian (Anabasis of Alexander). Despite the Persian attack, final victory goes to the Macedonians. Its only drawback for Alexander is that Darius again succeeds in escaping—though he will be assassinated a few months later by one of his own generals.

VICTORIES OF CONQUEST

OCTOBER 333: ISSUS

It's the middle of autumn in the heart of the Syrian mountains. The battle—the first one between Alexander and the Persian king Darius III—starts rapidly. Pinned down by the attack of the Macedonians shouting their war cry ("Alala, alala, alala"), the Persians are quickly overwhelmed, as is their leader. Pushed to the last entrenchment, Darius is forced to flee, abandoning on the way his war chariot, his gold, even his wife, mother, and children. After pursuing the fugitive for some time together with his soldiers, Alexander returns to the battlefield. "At midnight they advanced over the corpses. Alexander found the tent of Darius, entered it, and encamped there" (Pseudo-Callisthenes, The Romance of Alexander the Great). Taken prisoner, the mother, wife, and children of Darius are accorded due respect and receive the best of treatment. Better treatment than they got from Darius.

MAY 326 : JALALPUR

The fourth and final battle of the eastern expedition takes place on the shores of the Jhelum River (in present-day Pakistan). The adversary has changed: Darius is dead, and now Alexander wants to defeat the Indian ruler Porus. Porus throws all his forces into the battle: according to French historian Paul Faure there were 30,000 infantrymen and archers, not to mention more than one hundred war elephants. Menaced from two sides, the Indian sovereign defends himself in the best possible way. As at Gaugamela, the elephants inflict considerable damage on the Greeks. "Some of the Macedonians were trodden underfoot, armor and all, by the beasts and died, their bones crushed. Others were caught up by the elephants' trunks and, lifted on high, were dashed back down to the ground again, dying a fearful death. Many soldiers were pierced through by the tusks and died instantly, run through the whole body" (Diodorus Siculus, Universal History). Riding the tallest elephant, Porus courageously faces the Greeks. Wounded, exhausted after eight hours of harried fighting, he ends up by kneeling his elephant mount and surrendering to Alexander.

TAKING THE SHOW

ASSORTED CIVILIANS
Women and children, scholars and intellectuals, artists, merchants, even actors: thousands of these follow the army day after day. Their role: to entertain, to analyze each new area, to engage in trade. Simply by being around, these people help maintain the soldiers' morale and diminish their homesickness.

SOOTHSAYERS AND SEERS
They provide advice on plans to be adopted for battles. They base their predictions on the flight of birds, meteorological events, as well as examination of the internal organs of animals.

BAGGAGE TRAIN
These are the vehicles that carry weapons, armor, tents, food—three to four thousand wagons in total, which can be used when needed by the wounded or exhausted marchers, should they be lucky enough not to be abandoned along the way. Donkeys and mules also help with the hauling of supplies, and cattle are brought along on the journey.

MACEDONIA

BLACK SEA

ATHENS

MEDITERRANEAN
SEA

INTELLIGENCE
There are swarms of spies, many of them deserters from other armies, and their duties are varied. Some of them make maps, others do translating or study geography. In that regard, the most unusual are the men in charge of counting, one by one, the number of steps from one encampment to the next.

Euphrates River

Tigris River

ALEXANDRIA

ENGINEERS AND ARTILLERY
These number about 4,000 men, with engineers, mechanics, blacksmiths, and carpenters. Their creations—siege machines, cranes, grappling hooks—are of primary importance during sieges. Catapults, ballistae, and lithobolos are the main artillery pieces of the day.

BABYLONIA

Nile River

RED SEA

ALEXANDER
The Great can be found most often at the head of his cavalry.

Civilians, soldiers, women, children, artists, geographers—between 334 and 323 B.C. Alexander the Great brings with him on his conquests nearly 100,000 people (only half of them soldiers). They all take the same route: unexplored paths and roads, gates and passes. Moving ever forward, an entire city follows the Macedonian conqueror on his eastern adventure. Over the years, this long caravan discovers roads that will later be used by the

ON THE ROAD

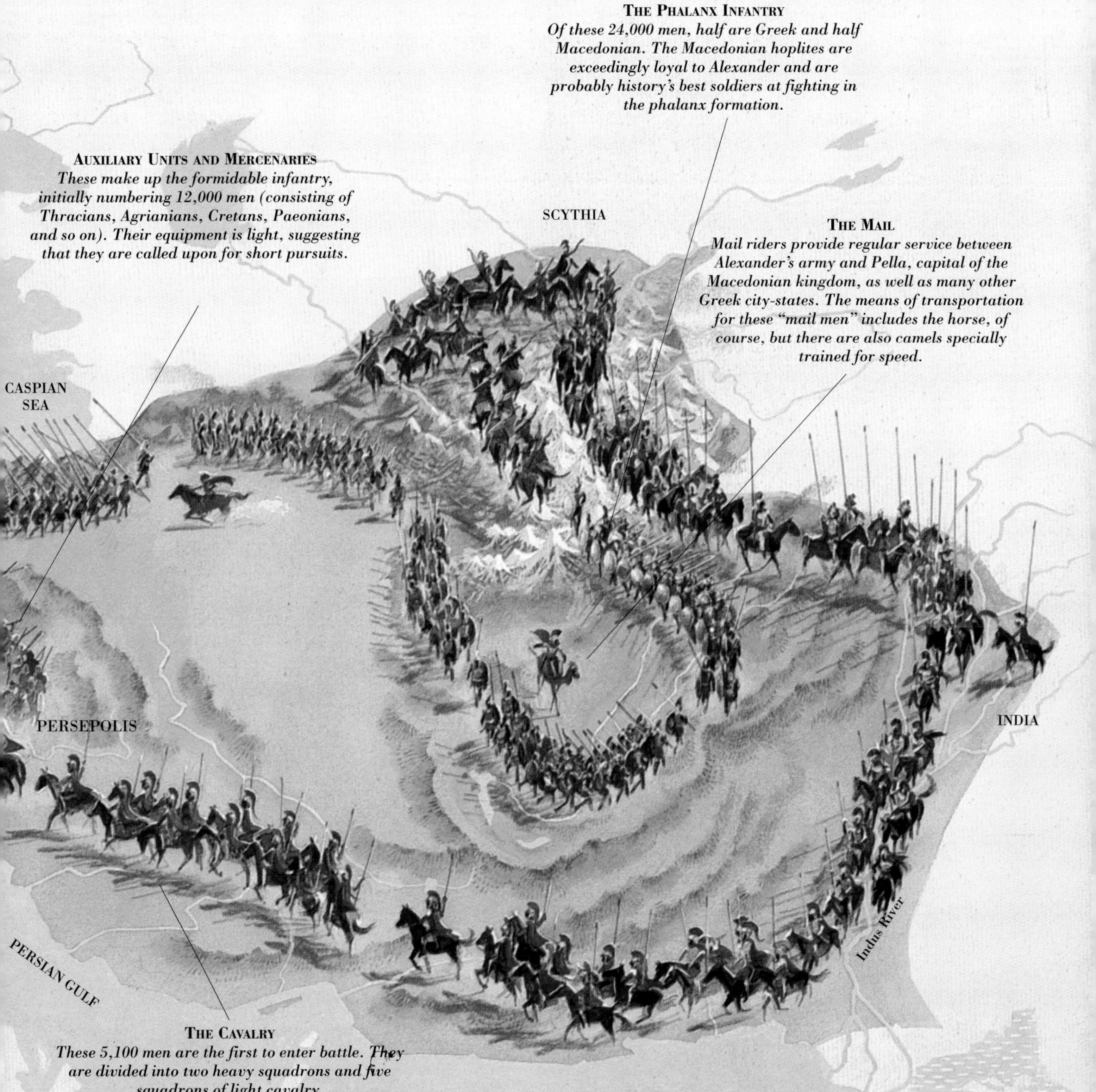

THE PHALANX INFANTRY
Of these 24,000 men, half are Greek and half Macedonian. The Macedonian hoplites are exceedingly loyal to Alexander and are probably history's best soldiers at fighting in the phalanx formation.

AUXILIARY UNITS AND MERCENARIES
These make up the formidable infantry, initially numbering 12,000 men (consisting of Thracians, Agrianians, Cretans, Paeonians, and so on). Their equipment is light, suggesting that they are called upon for short pursuits.

SCYTHIA

THE MAIL
Mail riders provide regular service between Alexander's army and Pella, capital of the Macedonian kingdom, as well as many other Greek city-states. The means of transportation for these "mail men" includes the horse, of course, but there are also camels specially trained for speed.

CASPIAN SEA

PERSEPOLIS

INDIA

Indus River

PERSIAN GULF

THE CAVALRY
These 5,100 men are the first to enter battle. They are divided into two heavy squadrons and five squadrons of light cavalry.

Romans, Genghis Khan, Marco Polo, even British soldiers during World War II. We're talking about 11,000 miles covered in eleven years of military campaigns—11,000 miles of marches, ambushes, sieges, all to gain an empire that will soon cover 3 million square miles. And all of this secured with the precious help of Athena, guardian of Athens and also goddess of war.

First marches under extreme heat, in Turkey, as well as the first battles against the Persians.

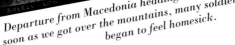

Departure from Macedonia heading east, spring of 334 B.C. As soon as we got over the mountains, many soldiers (including me) began to feel homesick.

Between Aria and Drangiana [to the west of today's Afghanistan]. After discovering the vast landscapes of Persian art, we explore Darius' empire— and meet herds of wild horses. Macedonia is definitely very far away.

Somewhere between Bactria and India [in the northern region of modern Pakistan]. After the terrible heat of the earlier march, the cold weather here freezes us to the bone.

SOLDIERS HAD A CAMERA?

Egypt: this is where our leader founded the city of Alexandria and consulted the god Ammon at the oasis of Siwah. The water of the Nile wasn't bad and refreshed all of us.

In Hyrcania [present-day Iran], we are continuously pursuing barbarians. They say it's a singular opportunity to discover Persian art, but who has the time!

On the shores of the Indus River, in 326. Exhausted, many of the soldiers refuse to undertake the conquest any further. The army begins its return by going down the river to the south.

Return of the heat, as we skirt along the Persian Gulf. The deserts, throughout the entire conquest, have given us much toil and tribulation; among these, the Gedrosian desert [present-day Pakistan] was without doubt the worst.

BARBARIAN?

Greek or barbarian? On several occasions during his conquests, Alexander the Great commits deeds that chroniclers and historians never cease to denounce. At Tyre, at the end of year 332, more than 6,000 men and women are enslaved. Some years later, when the army enters India, the number has greatly increased: some 80,000 slaves follow the military procession, feet and fists bound—human livestock that Greek tradesmen will soon buy.

Greek or barbarian? Between 334 and 323 B.C., the armies of Alexander the Great don't place too much value on human life. From Thebes to Tyre, Gaza to Sogdiana, from expeditions to incursions, the repression is bloody and sometimes goes beyond all expected severity. At Persepolis (in modern Iran), on the night of April 25, 330, after a dreadful orgy at the Macedonian headquarters, Alexander's men dash into the palace of Xerxes I (519-465 B.C.) and set it on fire. This is an utterly senseless act since the city has been in Macedonian hands for many months, and the Persian elite have submitted without resistance. In 327 in Massaga (in modern Pakistan), just after the Greek armies have entered India they are confronted with the ruler of a kingdom the size of Egypt. Alexander concludes a truce with their ruler, but when some of their soldiers bravely defend a city, Alexander waits until they have surrendered and then falls upon them "as they were marching away, and put them all to the sword" (Plutarch, *Lives*). So, Greek or barbarian? Alexander is a bit of both. The mind behind so many valuable administrative reforms, creator of cities, builder of roads, Alexander the Great also spreads terror along his way. But then who could ever believe that a conquest could be peaceful?

ALEXANDER'S RENDEZVOUS

Babylon, the end of October 331: at the head of his 47,000 veterans, Alexander enters the ancient city. The marching column passes the ramparts and enters the narrow streets of the city center. This is an intense and solemn moment. Babylon is called the "city of totality," "the divine gateway," and it gradually captivates the Macedonians. Like the sovereigns Hammurabi (fl. 1792-1750 B.C.) and Nebuchadnezzar (reigned 605-562 B.C.),

Alexander advances regally through the mythical city. Four or five times larger than Athens, this city is organized around a central ziggurat seven stories (300 feet) in height—the famous tower of Babel described in the Bible. At Babylon, however, the conqueror doesn't know he has a rendezvous with his own destiny. Beyond the architectural beauty of the urban districts, beyond the hanging gardens, beyond the processional way leading to the temple of the god Marduk, tight links will soon be formed between the Macedonian and this Mesopotamian city. Indeed, during the last months of Alexander's life, he and the city interest each other endlessly,

WITH DESTINY IN BABYLON

as if driven by a mutual fascination. A telling sign of this fascination with Babylon is that at the beginning of 323 Alexander selects this city as the burial place for his beloved friend Hephaestion, who is laid to rest in great style. Described in the ancient sources, Hephaestion's tomb is even more lavish than that of Alexander's own father, Philip. "Upon the foundation course were golden prows of warships in close order, two hundred and forty

in all . . . on the third level were carved a multitude of wild animals being pursued by hunters . . . the fifth showed lions and bulls alternating, also in gold . . . on top of all stood Sirens, hollowed out and able to conceal within them persons who sang a lament in mourning for the dead" (Diodorus Siculus, *Universal History*). After his friend's death, Alexander almost never leaves the city. Between April and May of 323, the man and the city seem to communicate with each another. Alexander feels at home in Babylon. It is in this very city that a few weeks later—on June 10, 323—Alexander will pass away after a period of slow agony.

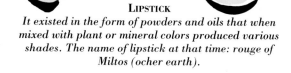

LIPSTICK

It existed in the form of powders and oils that when mixed with plant or mineral colors produced various shades. The name of lipstick at that time: rouge of Miltos (ocher earth).

CROSSBOW

It existed, and well before the Middle Ages this weapon wreaked much havoc in the hands of eastern armies.

PEPPER

It didn't exist. The Greeks were well acquainted with salt, however, which they obtained from the sea.

SUPPOSITORIES

They existed. Greek doctors, who specialized in traditional therapeutic treatments, often recommended them. What form did they have? Sadly, no one took the time to write down a description of one for posterity.

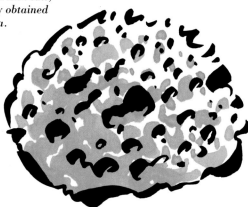

SPONGES

They existed; of course, we're talking about natural sponges, which Greek divers found in the sea. Sponges were used primarily for washing.

CHAIRS

These certainly existed and were surprisingly similar to those we sit on today.

WASN'T IN ALEXANDER'S DAY

OIL
It existed. The Greeks discovered it in Asia and used it for fuel.

NERVOUS DEPRESSION
It existed. Although rare, it was known to doctors because of the related suicidal tendencies it sometimes brought about. The philosopher Plato categorically condemned suicide as "cowardice unworthy of man."

BATHTUBS
They existed. The Greeks took several baths each day and used all kinds of tubs. Most bathtubs were located in public baths where washing was performed by pouring water over the body.

CHANGE PURSE
It existed, in a way, since some Greeks used their mouths as a change purse, holding small coins there and spitting them out as needed. That's precisely why Greek doctors strongly recommended regular oral hygiene.

PARASOL
It existed and was very similar to the hand-held ones we know today. The umbrella, however, had yet to come into being.

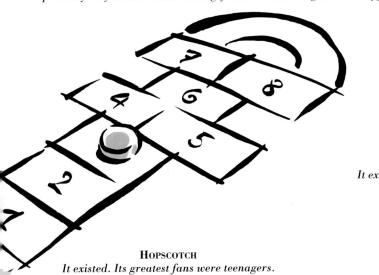

HOPSCOTCH
It existed. Its greatest fans were teenagers.

YO-YO
It existed, but not in the shape we know today.

WHEN SUPERMAN, BATMAN, AJAX, ODYSSEUS,

Comic books have not yet been invented, but that doesn't keep the Greeks from assigning supernatural powers to their heroes. Perseus, Agamemnon, and certainly Achilles, Odysseus, and Ajax—these heroes are well known to all the Greeks, sometimes influencing them as much as the gods. Herakles, who was a hero before becoming a member of the divine pantheon, is a shining example of the bridge the Greeks create between the realms of legend and religion. Odysseus and his long journey to get home to his island of Ithaca, Achilles and Paris, Jason and the Golden Fleece—what are the origins of the myths circulating in Greece at the time of Alexander the Great? It's difficult to say. One important source is the works of the epic poet Homer. First in the *Iliad* and then in the *Odyssey*, Homer recounts the adventures of Achilles and Odysseus as they

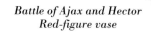

Battle of Ajax and Hector
Red-figure vase

AND SPIDERMAN WERE CALLED
AND ACHILLES

fight in the Trojan War. These great deeds, fantastic yet so colorful, soon spread across the entire Greek mainland and even beyond, due to the many wandering storytellers. A common motif of these tales is the struggle of man to impose his will against his fate. Achilles is the foremost example. He is the son of the mortal Peleus and the marine nymph Thetis, who sought to make him invulnerable by dipping him as a baby in the River Styx (but she forgot the part of his foot she was holding him by, leaving one mortal spot, his heel). Sure enough, he dies when struck by an arrow from Paris' bow that pierces only his heel. Which only goes to show that even 2,300 years before Spiderman, Superman, and Batman, the superheroes of the day have their little soft spots.

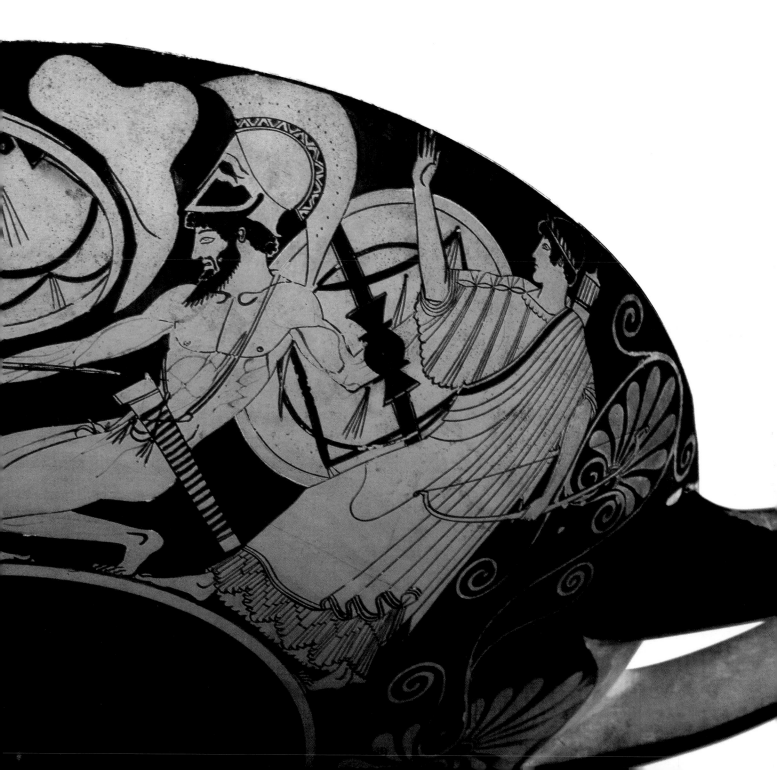

LET THE MASKS COME DOWN:

How can one justify a military campaign that takes people farther and farther from home? How can one explain the need for endless marches that soldiers find harder and harder to endure? Having set off to conquer the Persia of Darius III, Alexander the Great calls on his army to continue eastward. After Lycia, Phrygia, Syria, and Egypt, the Greek forces drive on into Babylonia, Media, Parthia, Bactria—it never stops. Despite the death of Darius III in 330, despite the submission of Persia, Alexander continues to launch his cavalry and infantry on assaults of well-fortified fortresses. He reaches Sogdiana, enters India, and then, exhilarated, he suddenly starts dreaming of a universal kingdom over which he will reign as absolute master: there's no limit to his ambition.

Realizing that there is no end in sight, people start to grumble. They want to return home to their wives, children, and families. Each time Alexander faces them courageously, appealing to their honor, to the loyalty they have pledged, to the wealth the conquest could yet bring to them. But his most compelling argument is that the Greeks must conquer the East in order to avenge the humiliation of their ancestors during the Persian Wars (beginning of fifth century B.C.) as well as to ensure that the eastern Greek cities are protected against Persian attacks. A clever politician and first-rate actor, Alexander takes time to personally motivate each unit of his army: "And as he rode past the ranks, he addressed the soldiers in different terms, such as were appropriate to the feelings of each. The Macedonians, victors in Europe in so many wars, who had set out to subjugate Asia and the farthest parts of the Orient, were reminded of their old-time valor . . . Whenever he came to Greek troops, he reminded them that it was by these nations that war had been made upon their country through the insolence of the first Darius . . . As to the Illyrians and the Thracians, men accustomed to live by plunder, he bade them look upon the enemies' army, gleaming with gold and purple, bearing booty rather than arms" (Quintus Curtius, *History of Alexander*).

But the men do not follow him to the ends of the earth. After the death of Darius III in 330 the army resolves that it has concluded its "Hellenic crusade"—their job is done. On the shores of the Hydaspes River (India), in the middle of the summer of 326, the army refuses for the last time. The confrontation with their leader is terrible: to Alexander, turning back means retreating. But at last "the cries and lamentations of his soldiers" (Plutarch, *Lives*) persuade him. The great motivator has lost a decisive battle.

ALEXANDER THE GREAT MOTIVATOR

Masks from Greek tragedy and comedy

Problem: Can one say that every projection preserves the ratio of two collinear vectors?

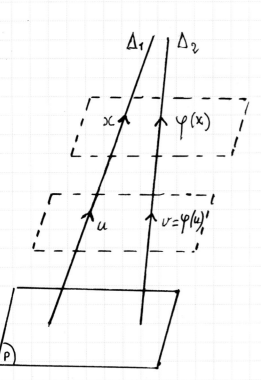

Let there be 2 straight lines Δ_1 and Δ_2 and a plane P which intersects them.

Let $V\Delta_1$ be the ensemble of vectors that are parallel to Δ_1 and $V\Delta_2$ the ensemble of vectors parallel to Δ_2. We know that $V\Delta_1$ and $V\Delta_2$ are vectorial spaces. Let phi be the projector on $V\Delta_2$ parallel to P. The restriction of phi on $V\Delta_1$ is then a bijective application of $V\Delta_1$ over $V\Delta_2$. Therefore this restriction of phi is an isomorphism for the vectorial summation of $V\Delta_1$ on $V\Delta_2$.

Let u be a unitary vector on $V\Delta_1$ and v a unitary vector on $V\Delta_2$, such that v=phi (u).

Let muv be the measure in $V\Delta_2$. Let us consider the function f of v in R: f=muvophi.

The restriction of f to $V\Delta_1$ being composed of two bijections is abijection of $V\Delta 1$ over R.

- Moreover: f(u)=muv[pi(u)]=muv(v)=1.

- But we know that phi and muv are both two of the homomorphies for the summation,

then: f(x+x')=muv[phi(x+x')]=muv[phi(x)] + muv[phi(x')]=f(x)+f(x')

If x and u are in the same direction, then their projections y(x) and v are in the same direction and f(x) epsilon R.+. Therefore, for any x of $V\Delta 1$, f(x) is the gauge of x when u is taken as a unity: (V_x $V\Delta 1$) muv(x) = muv[phi(x)].

If one denotes by alpha this common gauge, then:

    alpha=mu(x)—>x=alpha u

    alpha=muv[phi(x)]—-->phi(x)=alpha v=alpha phi(u).

Consequently: for any real number alpha and vector u:

$\boxed{}$

SURPRISE QUIZ:
PROVE THE THEOREM OF THALES

In Ionia, some three centuries before the birth of Alexander the Great and 700 years before Christ, a new scientific attitude based on reason comes into being. The progenitor of this new "philosophical" movement is Thales of Miletus (624-548 B.C.). The son of an illustrious Milesian family, he is fascinated by politics, economics, and astronomy—and he is later ranked among the seven great wise men of antiquity. In his youth Thales stands out because of his intense interest in the world: not satisfied to be a patient observer of the environment, Thales tries continuously to modify it and thus tame nature. Could the ships of Ionian merchants ever cross the seas without impediment? Because their precarious journey cannot be left to chance, Thales determines which stars will allow the sailors to direct themselves and steer their ships. Greek peasants are interested in figuring out the size of their fields, and once again the Milesian philosopher comes to the rescue and invents a type of geometrical calculation to do just that. The originality of this system lies in the fact that it is grounded in everyday objects and events rather than abstract theory.

Thales of Miletus is the father of rational scientific thought. An inventor before his time, a Cartesian before Descartes, the Milesian philosopher brings about a drastic change in the way people perceive nature. Relying on experience, he develops an abstract method based on principles that will later inspire mathematicians (Pythagoras), philosophers (Aristotle), and also astronomers. His legacy includes the school created by Hippocrates, a faithful disciple of Thales' principles, who in the fifth century B.C. lays the basis for medicine at a time when magic or religious practices are traditionally used to cure the sick. His method contains two main steps—to examine (this is the prognosis) and to diagnose (the diagnosis)—that help him prescribe correct remedies.

Twenty-seven centuries later these principles are still in use. Scientist, wise man, and scholar, Thales of Miletus is the father of mathematics and geometry. You may not be familiar with his name, but his theorem still terrorizes thousands of college students daily. "Let A, B, and C be three points on the straight line D . . ." Thales got the idea for this principle—in which many straight lines are brought together by parallel projections—after closely studying a spider's web!

Who would have thought spiders could be so deep?

THEOREM OF THALES

Let D1 and D2 be two intersecting straight lines.
A, B, C on D_1.
One draws through A, B, and C 3 parallel straight lines to D2. They intersect D1 in A_1, B_1 and C_1.
then:
$$\frac{AB}{BC} = \frac{A_1B_1}{B_1C_1}$$
The ratio of the projections is preserved.

We're counting on you to find the formula and write it in the square provided on the opposite page (just kidding).

GREEK

Kept on the fringe of society and excluded from citizenship, the Greek woman has always attracted the interest of historians and chroniclers. We cannot rely on the prejudiced opinion of Aristotle, according to whom "the relationship between males and females is by nature one of the superior to the inferior, of the governor and the governed" (see our interview with Aristotle on pages 62-63). While not having the privileges of men, Greek women do live active and vital lives. They even have a special place of their own, the gynaiconitis, where men are forbidden. In these apartments, women attend to the cleansing and beautification of their bodies. They perform a variety of activities, such as bathing, hair removal, and hair coloring. Within this exclusive world women speak of fashion, practice the art of refined manners, and try on rings, diadems, and other jewelry—Greek refinement knows no limits!

BEAUTY PRODUCTS: NATURAL MAKEUP

Like precious stones and toiletry items, beauty products are extremely varied. Powdered iris from Elis or Cyzicus, perfumes made from marjoram and apples from Cos, rose extract from Phaselis—women certainly have a choice! One of the many products that are obtained naturally is makeup. Its purpose is to brighten and animate the face; makeup can improve a very pale complexion (try saturnine red), emphasize the eyes (paint the eyebrows and eyelids with antimony), or accentuate the teeth (lipstick, of course).

FASHION

FASHIONABLE ATHENIAN WOMEN PARADE WITH CRICKETS

Crickets and cicadas are particularly popular with the Greeks. After catching them, Athenian women keep them in a gold cage and take them out occasionally and place them in their hair. This is the height of fashion: what could be better than strolling down the street accompanied by the insect's song attracting attention everywhere?

JEWELRY: THE SNAKE'S SHINING EYES

Athenian women treasure rings and, above all, necklaces. Necklaces are made of pearls, precious metals like gold and silver, and also several types of precious stone (emeralds, rubies, garnets). As for bracelets, they often symbolize an animal, such as the snake. Snake bracelets are made to wrap around the arm, with the creature's tail twisting toward the end in a graceful movement. The most remarkable aspect of this kind of jewelry is the head, soldered to the rest of the body, which has eyes made of precious stones.

THE CHIC AND PRACTICAL "READY-TO-WEAR"

Greek clothing consists of drapery derived from a rectangular piece of cloth. Greek women prefer most of all a garment called the peplos, which is secured at the shoulders and serves as both tunic and cape. Because this garment provides only minimal cover for one side of the body, the playwright Euripides calls the young girls who wear it "exhibitionists of the thigh" (Andromache). His opinion makes more sense when you remember that Greek women—like Greek men— never wear any kind of underwear.

ROXANA
Daughter of a Bactrian nobleman, Oxyartes, Roxana (meaning "the light") marries Alexander the Great during the winter of 327 B.C. The ceremony takes place at Bactra (modern Afghanistan), before the conqueror resumes his conquest in the direction of India. Alexander and Roxana meet again, however, and in December 324 the Persian woman gives the Macedonian a son whom he never knows: Alexander Aegus (323-310).

PARYSATIS
The marriage of Alexander the Great with the daughter of Artaxerxes III takes place in March 324. The place of the ceremony is the city of Susa, where a sumptuous and symbolic banquet with 9,000 guests is staged in hope of establishing peace between Greeks and Persians. Parysatis does not produce an heir for the Macedonian throne.

In his biography of Alexander the Great, Plutarch attributes to him the remark that "women are the torment of the eyes." These are certainly surprising words for a man who has little interaction with women. Of course, following the example of his father, Philip, who married no fewer than seven times, Alexander marries three times during the course of his life: Roxana in 327 and Parysatis and Statira in March 324. But these are marriages of convenience rather than marriages of the heart. In fact, all three of his marriages have a hidden political significance, for it seems that each time the marriage is intended to symbolize the harmony between Greeks and Persians. Such marriages are not much different from military conquests and are governed by logic, not the heart. In reality, Alexander the Great has only one great love during his short life, and that is for a man: Hephaestion.

ONE GREAT LOVE

HEPHAESTION
The Macedonian king's childhood friend Hephaestion accompanies Alexander throughout his conquest of the east. Soon Hephaestion gains many honorary titles: chief general of the companion cavalry (hipparch), chief of the Persian court (chiliarch, or grand vizier), and he is Alexander's most trusted dignitary.

STATIRA
Daughter of the Persian ruler Darius III, Statira marries Alexander the Great on the same day that he marries Parysatis (when you're the Great, you can do what you want). Actually, the king of Macedonia marries them one after the other. Both women are from the nobility of the east. This union produces no children.

The relationship between these two men—homosexuality was not looked down upon at that time—starts very early, certainly from the time of their adolescence. If one believes most of the chroniclers, over the years Hephaestion became Alexander's closest confidant, the very shadow of the Macedonian conqueror. "He had more freedom than anyone else in admonishing Alexander, a privilege which he nevertheless used in such a manner that it seemed rather to be allowed by the king than claimed by himself. He was of the same age, but of larger stature," writes Quintus Curtius, who also relates a telling event in their friendship. Following the battle of Issus (October 333) Darius III's wife and mother, taken prisoner, confuse Hephaestion with Alexander. When the error is pointed out, the queen throws herself at Alexander's feet, begging his pardon. The king, taking her hand and raising her to her feet, says, "You were not mistaken, mother; for this man, too, is Alexander."

BLACK BROTH
Stew of pork with a blood sauce seasoned with salt and vinegar. It is served with aromatic herbs and small vegetables.

YOU EAT WITH YOUR HANDS

Oh, how the Mediterranean influences the culinary art! The contemporaries of Alexander the Great are blessed by the sea and its appetizing fish and seafood. Barbel, perch, minnow, octopus, lobster, and shrimp, nothing escapes them. But that's not to say they go without meat. From donkeys to hedgehogs, as well as foxes and dogs (that's right!), everything is up for grabs. Clearly, the Greeks have strong stomachs.

The staple element in the cuisine of this period is maza, a sort of barley flour that was at first grilled, but later was used for baking bread.

What do they drink besides water? Mainly red wine, although white wine is also consumed. The red has a high alcohol content that can reach 20 percent. The most famous wines of this time come from Thasos, Chios, and Lesbos. Other drinks are rather rare, with the exception of palm wine, a foul-tasting brew made with fermented honey.

The Greeks of Alexander's day are also familiar with goat cheese as well as pastries (which they invented), vegetable appetizers, and various condiments, all in all a very diversified cuisine. The only drawback is that they eat with their hands. But then it's true that there are fewer dishes to wash in this way, and it's a lot more fun.

100%
Olive oil
for medicine

100%
Olive oil
against cold

100%
Olive oil
as a lubricant

100%
Olive oil
for the body

The Greeks possess a magic potion: olive oil. This product is everywhere in the world of Alexander the Great. First of all, it is used in medicine; according to Hippocrates, specialists warmly recommend it for disinfecting, healing wounds, and even loosening lumps of earwax! Olive oil is also on hand at sporting activities, in stadiums and gymnasiums, where athletes spread it all over their bodies to protect them against bad weather. Soldiers find it wonderfully useful, and aboard Alexander's warships olive oil is used for the maintenance of metal parts and serves as an

IN-ONE PRODUCT

100%
Olive oil
for the table

100%
Olive oil
for religious rites

100%
Olive oil
for textiles

100%
Olive oil
for lighting

all-purpose lubricant. The trusty oil is equally essential in everyday life, for hygiene (perfume, baths), in food (over raw vegetables and bread and in meat sauces), in religious rites (called libations), on textiles (to preserve clothing), and even for domestic illumination (lamp fuel)—this is a product that no Greek can do without. The numbers speak for themselves: out of the nearly 16 gallons of oil used annually by each Greek, only one quarter is used in meals. So if you're looking for a magic potion, go no farther than the olive oil section of your local grocery store.

EXCLUSIVE: ARISTOTLE TALKS TO

Aristotle is a man who needs no introduction. Born in 384 B.C., the famous scholar and philosopher has agreed to join us for a discussion of some of the important ideas in his works. He will also speak to us about Alexander the Great, who was his pupil for many years.

⑤ : *Aristotle, thank you for agreeing to answer some of our questions. We'll get right to the point. It's said that you have never been kind to the feminine gender; some go so far as to consider you a misogynist. How do you answer these allegations?*

Aristotle (very seriously): Among animals the relationship between male and female is by nature one of a superior to an inferior, of the governor and the governed; this principle also applies to humankind.

⑤ : *So you believe in a certain similarity between animal species, which you have deeply studied in your works on biology, and the human species. In other words, you really set man—the head of the family—on a pedestal?*

Aristotle: The head of the family exercises his authority over his wife and children knowing that they, too, are equally free. Men by nature are more prone to rule than women (excluding some exceptions that go against nature), in the same way as age and maturity are more capable than youth and inexperience. You may recall that our great Sophocles has something to say on this, and his words concerning women reflect a general truth: "Silence gives the proper grace to women."

⑤ : *Well, let's move on to another subject. We all know about your works of philosophy, but many* would be surprised to learn that you've written about everything from botany to meteorology. Let's take politics, for example. On several occasions you deal with different types of government, and in particular with democracy. Can you tell us more about this topic?

Aristotle: The basic principle of any democratic regime is freedom. This is what you usually hear— that only in this system do the people enjoy true freedom. Of course, that is the goal of any democracy. But one of the basic factors of freedom is the ability to govern and also to be governed in turn.

⑤ : *So you think that democracy is only one of the solutions possible?*

Aristotle: The multitude is the best judge!

⑤ : *Probably so. Anyway, does believing that make you condemn other forms of government? For instance, what's your opinion of royalty?*

Aristotle: Well, here's a good question: who shall be the sovereign of a city? Evidently it can either be the general population, the rich, the important people, or a single person, the best of all being a tyrant. In my opinion, royalty is one of the best institutions. The being who, due to his intelligence, is able to provide for everything is a leader and master by nature.

⑤ : *You certainly are familiar with royalty. For six years—from 342 to 336 B.C.—you lived at the Macedonian court near King Philip II. For three of those years you were the tutor of the future Alexander the Great. Are there any wise sayings that you tried to get across to him?*

Aristotle: "Know thyself," meaning, "Recognize that you are only a man"; "Nothing in excess," meaning, "Don't act like a god"; "You can answer like another, but misfortune will follow," meaning, "Stay in your place, if not you're sure to regret it."

⑤ : *It is also said that you were in touch with the Macedonian during his long voyage toward the east. What advice did you give the vanquisher of Darius III?*

Aristotle (struggling to remember): The regent must unite in himself two qualities that are of the utmost importance: he must be loved by his people and be admired for his actions. He should also remember the three things that make rulers famous: the first one is good legislation, the second the science of war, the third is the foundation of cities.

: *Alexander seems to have followed your advice, and he certainly did well at war and founding cities. But what about when he had to face increasing hostility from his own side (we mean particularly the mutiny of his soldiers). What did you tell him then?*

Aristotle: When Greeks are involved, beware to listen attentively to the denunciations of informers who would like to destroy the reputation of others in your eyes. Do not be angry against those whom you find are trying to emulate you, seeking to match you in dignity and grandiose projects. Do not offend anyone by giving an order that would make you a master instead of a regent, a hated tyrant instead an admired king. Some people think that it is not important if a sovereign is feared and that he doesn't need to heed the law: this will obviously make matters worse.

 : *At one point some chroniclers and biographers advanced the idea that you disagreed with Alexander. You were not in favor of the king's unification politics, although you continued to give him valuable advice. Can you remember some of your suggestions?*

Aristotle (again having difficulty remembering): I said, Alexander, your supreme power will be more glorious and honorable if you take good care of people's well-being. It is better to exert your power on free and noble people than to dominate slaves, even though very numerous. Know that any offenses to the dignity of a free man is more cruel than physical harm or loss of wealth. Remember that time passes over everything, distorting events, erasing memorable achievements, and destroying memories, except those that are engraved by love onto the hearts of men—those will be passed on from generation to generation.

 : *Aristotle, to finish off this interview, let's get back to your opinion of slavery. Similar to your ideas on women, the notions you develop in some of your writings concerning slaves seem to be quite different from ours. Is this true?*

Aristotle (nodding his head): To command and to obey are not only inevitable things but are also useful; immediately after their birth some people are destined to obey while others to command. That is why a slave is not only a servant of a master, but completely belongs to him.

 : *What we still can't get over is that you do not have a negative image of slavery.*

Aristotle: It seems natural to me that there are people who are free and others who are slaves, and thus the servile condition is both advantageous and fair. Some are strong for the required tasks, while others—straight of stature and unsuitable for such activities—are destined for political life (which is divided between the occupations of war and peace).

 : *You seem very sure of your opinion. In your work* Politics, *you almost come to the point of doubting that the slave could be virtuous—and we all know the importance you place throughout your works on this notion of virtue, the fundamental condition of happiness.*

Aristotle (obviously moved): First of all, concerning the slaves, one should consider the question: besides his qualities as a servant, does the slave have another virtue of higher value, such as moderation, courage, justice, or does he have no benefits except his ability to work? This is a complicated issue: if slaves do have personal virtue, in what way do they differ from free men? If they don't have virtue, then it would be strange to consider them human beings and thus able to participate in reasoning. Almost the same question can be raised concerning women and children, something we discussed at the very beginning of this interview.

 : *Thank you, Aristotle. This has been very informative.*

WHEN
MONSTERS
PROWLED
THE EARTH

For young Greeks of the fourth century B.C., falling asleep to the rhythm of Dionysus' Indian conquest as described by the historian Ctesias, India is nothing more than a land of the imagination. In that faraway place one thousand and one surprises await all voyagers: ants as big as foxes, bearded parrots fluent in Greek and Indian, swarms of oysters—it is truly an enchanted place. Therefore, as you might expect, when the soldiers of Alexander go down the Indus River in order to return to Persepolis—following their military conquests of 325—they do not hide their fear. As the Greeks make their way along the coast, they report sighting very strange animals. One night they camp by a waterhole: "I [Alexander] gave orders to make camp, prepare to rest, and light a fire. Toward the third hour of the night, under

the bright moon and stars, wild beasts came out of the forest to go to the watering place. There were scorpions a cubit long, vipers in the sand, some of them white, some red...some men perished fighting them. Afterward four-legged beasts appeared: lions larger than our bulls at home...wild boars larger than the lions with teeth a cubit in length, lynxes, leopards, tigers, scorpions, elephants, wild oxen, bull elephants...and barefooted men with six feet...We drove some away with our iron weapons and we set fire to the woods. The serpents ran into the fire. There were those we stamped on, those we killed with our swords, but most of them were burnt. Shaken by fear and terrible dread, we stood wondering at their varied forms. And suddenly a wild animal came that was larger than any elephant, with one horn, and it wanted to attack us...in its eagerness to hurt the men it fell into the flames. Then it ran into the army and killed twenty-six men at once. Some of our brave men struck down and slew the one-horned beast. And 1,300 men were hardly able to drag him away from the place...when it was day, these animals all went away" (Pseudo-Callisthenes, *The Romance of Alexander the Great*). Are Alexander's men hallucinating, or are these beasts real? The truth is that storytellers can't resist embellishing a good story, and this one has clearly passed through several generations of "improvers."

How many? Is it 32? 42? Or perhaps 72? During his twelve years of active conquest, Alexander the Great founds a large number of cities bearing his name. From Alexandria-in-Susiana (Charax) to Alexandria-of-the-Caucasus, from Alexandria in Arachosia to Alexandria-the-Furthest (Eschate), the Macedonian conqueror persistently leaves his personal stamp on the landscape he traverses. His goal is to erect islands of Greek culture all along his route, almost as if he were a little child dropping marbles behind him so as not to lose his way. Among all the Alexandrias, one city—grand and magnificent—will survive over the centuries: the Alexandria in Egypt.

"It is reported that when the king had marked out the circuit of the new city with peeled barley, as is the custom of the Macedonians, flocks of birds flew to the spot and ate the barley; and when that was regarded by many as a bad omen, the seers predicted that a great number of newcomers would dwell in that city, and that it would furnish sustenance to many lands" (Quintus Curtius, *History of Alexander*).

Alexandria in Egypt, a mythical city. Officially founded on January 20, 331 B.C., on a site with land that is not very favorable but chosen for its strategic location. Soon after, the city quickly begins to develop, both commercially and demographically. Being the

ALEXANDRIAS OF ALEXANDER

point of passage for all goods leaving Egypt for the Mediterranean world, the city is a symbol of variety on every level (cultural, commercial, historical).

After Alexander dies (and according to ancient sources is buried near the city), Alexandria continues to prosper. Starting in 290 B.C., the Alexandrians build a lighthouse on the island of Pharos. Designed to provide light to guide maritime vessels into port, this monument stands tall with titanic proportions. In antiquity it is hailed as one of the Seven Wonders of the World, and its height is later said to inspire the style of Arabian minarets. Its ruins, lost for centuries, have only recently been rediscovered by archaeologists. The city is also famous for its library. This structure is said to have housed up to 700,000 works on papyrus—a genuine data bank of the culture from that period! Through its prosperity and fame, Alexandria continues the work begun by Alexander beyond his lifetime. Thanks to Alexander, Greek culture continues to prosper and spread.

One of the seven wonders of the ancient world: the lighthouse of Alexandria in Egypt.

THEY TOOK UP TO FOUR BATHS
EACH DAY
YET NEVER WASHED!

Although they live in a far different time, the ancient Greeks' customs are similar to our own: in the Greece of Alexander the Great, people take at least one bath before the sun sets. This ancestral ritual is unalterable, and it is sometimes repeated as many as three or four times in the same day. Is this an obsession with cleanliness or a ridiculous eccentricity? Actually, neither. In fact, far from being considered as a means of washing, the bath water has two functions in classical Greece: one spiritual and one medical.

Greek fresco depicting a
rich woman being
bathed by her servants

Water is the element of divine purification. Sophocles, the great playwright of the fifth century B.C., referred to this property of water many times in his works, particularly at the end of his tragedy *Oedipus at Colonus*. Exhausted, nearing death, the hero has a final request, his very last desire: "He strips off his filthy rags, and after raising his voice he asks his daughters to bring him, from where they could, fresh water for a bath and his libations."

Water is an instrument of regeneration. The Greeks use water to "wash" some of their statues, and also their deceased. "We bathe the body in a bath which purifies, then we burn the remains in fresh-cut branches, and erect a tall tomb by spreading earth above it," writes Sophocles in his *Antigone*.

The famous Tomb of the Diver at Paestum. The painting has an impressive realism.

An invigorating element, the divine water has the role of renewing what we would call today the soul, something beyond hygiene or the simple cleanliness of the body. But if water is useful to the spirit, it also constitutes a central element for the "machine that is the human body." In the fifth century B.C., in his famous treatise *Air, Water, Earth*, the doctor Hippocrates presents an erudite theory concerning the basic healing role of the bath. For cases of hemorrhage the doctor prescribes soaking the head in cold water; he says that sponge baths calm and relax; and claims that a complete body bath will heal hysteria. At this time doctors are very precise about the conditions under which baths should be taken. They agree that all must be done "by the book," with proper vessels (tripods for pouring water, basins, cauldrons, pitchers, bathtubs); experienced assistants; a room with fresh air; and a generous amount of water, including some to be sprinkled over the body.

Faithful to these principles, Alexander the Great himself takes several baths a day throughout his life. Perhaps by chance or possibly as a sort of last wish, it is near water that the exhausted Macedonian conqueror awaits his death in the month of June 323. "Next day he bathed again, and sacrificed the appointed sacrifices . . . he bathed in the evening . . . next day he was carried again to the house near the bathing place" (Arrian, *Anabasis of Alexander*). Does Alexander attempt with this last effort to come closer to the gods? Perhaps . . .

AN ANCIENT ROLL CALL: FAMOUS FOLK

CICERO
(106-43 B.C.)

After Alexander. A contemporary of Julius Caesar, Marcus Tullius Cicero is a Roman politician and orator with a strong background in Greek rhetoric. After the debut of his career at the age of 25 as a lawyer, he becomes quaestor in Sicily in 75 B.C. and later governor. A man of rare honesty and integrity, always sincere in his actions, this eclectic philosopher publishes many essays, including his ardent Philippics, orations against Marc Antony, would-be successor to Caesar. He is assassinated in 43 B.C.

CLEOPATRA
(69-30 B.C.)

After Alexander. The queen of Egypt between 51 and 30 B.C., the daughter of Ptolemy XII Auletes and wife of her own brother, Ptolemy XIII, Cleopatra also lives during Caesar's time. The famous queen is said to bear him a son, Cesarion, in the hope of reestablishing the supremacy of Ptolemaic Egypt in the eastern Mediterranean. Following Caesar's assassination, Cleopatra falls in love with his would-be successor, Marc Anthony, and successfully involves him in her idealistic plans to create a powerful empire. Defeated by the Roman general Octavian (the future emperor Augustus), the two lovers commit suicide. In 30 B.C. Cleopatra allows herself to be bitten by an asp and dies at the age of 39.

THE VENUS OF MILO
(FIRST CENTURY B.C.)

After Alexander. Throughout antiquity, many statues are carved of Venus, the most famous surviving example being the marble Venus of Milo. Discovered in 1820 on the Greek island of Melos, this statue is exhibited at the Louvre in Paris and is one of the most visited masterpieces of Western art, much like the Mona Lisa by Leonardo da Vinci. Of course, Venus is the goddess of love, a Roman deity equivalent to the Greek goddess Aphrodite. Alexander the Great is familiar with stories about Aphrodite, including those in which she has love affairs with Ares, god of war. Beauty and war: to Alexander, the combination probably seems reasonable.

HERODOTUS
(484-420 B.C.)

Before Alexander. Born at Halicarnassus in the fifth century B.C., this Greek historian and traveler-geographer undertakes great expeditions in Asia Minor, Egypt (where he travels up the Nile), as well as Europe. Called the Father of History, he elaborates his experiences from his long voyages across the world in a book entitled The History. Written in Athens where the historian finally settles down, its nine sections are filled with descriptions of different peoples, cities, and cultures, including a passage about the tower of Babel (in Babylon), which will be a source of inspiration for many later scholars.

BEFORE AND AFTER ALEXANDER

SOPHOCLES
(C. 496-406 B.C.)

Before Alexander. An Athenian citizen born near Athens, Sophocles is one of the greatest tragic Greek playwrights. Having entered the theater around 468 B.C., he wins an award against the well-known playwright Aeschylus in his first competition (at that time plays are judged in contests). This event heralds Sophocles' magnificent success, for throughout his career he never receives anything below second place and wins first place twenty times. His most famous surviving works are Oedipus Rex, Ajax, Antigone, *and* Philoctetes.

HOMER
(NINTH CENTURY B.C.)

Before Alexander. Homer was probably born on the Ionian island of Smyrna (although no fewer than seven cities claim the honor of being his birthplace). It is said that he was blind. A great literary figure, Homer is the author of two epic poems that will have a great impact on the entire civilization of Greece: the Iliad *and the* Odyssey. *Focusing on two Greek heroes, Achilles and Odysseus, these works are known by everybody at the time of Alexander the Great and exert a great influence not only on philosophers and writers but also over daily life.*

PLATO
(428-347 B.C.)

Just before Alexander. Born in Athens, disciple of Heraclitus and close friend and student of Socrates, Plato is the first Greek philosopher whose works have been preserved. Founder of a famous school where philosophy is taught, the Academy (in Athens), he imparts his wisdom during long conversations. His most renowned works are the Republic *and the* Laws.

SANTA CLAUS

Long after Alexander. The old gentleman with the white beard and red tunic begins life as Saint Nicholas, patron saint of children and sailors and credited with various miracles, such as restoring to life three boys who'd been chopped up and pickled in brine by a butcher. The English in colonial New York adopt him from the Dutch (Santa Claus is a contraction of the Dutch Sinterklaas). Clement Clarke Moore's poem "A Visit from St. Nicholas," first published on December 23, 1823, gives a mighty boost to the former saint's popularity.

71

ASIAN OR GREEK, THE WAY OF THINKING

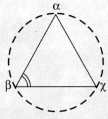

With Thales and Pythagoras, the Greeks laid the foundation of geometry

With the invasion of Alexander the Great and his armies into the East, not only did two civilizations confront each other, but also two systems of thought, with two radically different conceptions of the universe.

The Greeks are consumed with mastering the world. Philosophy, mathematics, geometry, physics, chemistry, biology, medicine, psychology, politics, economy—all the sciences are born in Greece starting in the sixth and continuing in the fifth centuries B.C., and they all aim toward proposing a unified system based on knowledge and reason. A famous philosopher who tackles the problem of scientific knowledge is Plato (428-347 B.C.). In his work the *Timaeus*, the founder of the Academy presents a deductive method (requiring the use of logic) based on definition, argument, and axiom. He attempts to make mathematics the language of cosmology, meaning the study of the universe. According to Plato, all natural sciences depend on

mathematics and geometry, so that man can master the world around him through knowledge and method. What becomes of Greek religion in all this? Even though religious beliefs remain popular at the time of Alexander, it is undeniable that the new rationalism makes them lose ground little by little.

IS DEFINITELY NOT THE SAME

scientific knowledge but to deal with the forces that emerge from it. One does not tame energy, one uses it. There is no separation between "scientific" reality and "sacred" reality: everything derives from the gods, imaginary things and magic being in the forefront. This explains the importance given by the Asians to astrology.

Greco-Buddhist art of Gandhara[1]

In the East, even the sciences seem to be linked to the divine! In fact, Asian mathematics are based on personal experience rather than analysis and theory.

So even in the time of Alexander the Great, it is possible to see vast philosophical differences between West and East.

Twenty-three centuries later we find once again the same separation between these two universes.

1. Located astride the middle Indus River, Gandhara developed a noted school of sculpture based on Buddhist thought blended with Greek elements first brought there by Alexander the Great.

Everything is different in the East. While Greek thinking seems to rely on a scientific approach, Asian thinking (meaning that of the Persians and Indians) is influenced by religion and ethics. For the subjects of Darius, the point is not to master the world through

ALEXANDER FINDS
RELIGION

"We, the Brahmans, gymnosophists, send greetings to the man who is called Alexander. Know that it is useless to come attack us, for there is nothing to take away from us. What we possess cannot be acquired by war, there is no need for bravery or battle. Rather, come to us in love; perhaps you will learn who we are."

—"Which is more powerful, death or life?" Alexander asked the wise Brahmans.

—"Life, because the rays of the sun are strongest at sunrise, weakest at evening toward sunset."

—"Of all the animals, which is the most cunning?"

—"Man."

—"Why is this?"

—"Look at yourself. See how many animals you have brought along with you in order to carry off all the other animals you capture."

—"What is a king?"

—"Someone who always wants more, who exercises his power unfairly, who is ready to grasp all opportunities to acquire gold. A king is a momentary success."

—"What is the sweetest thing in creation?"

—"Love that comes from the heart."

—"And what is the most bitter?"

—"Envy and hate."

(Pseudo-Callisthenes, *The Romance of Alexander the Great*)

Entering the forests of India in March 326 B.C. Alexander meets many native populations with diverse faiths. Among these are the wise Brahmans, visionary ascetics (gymnosophists) who regard life as punishment. Alexander is intrigued by these people who seem completely detached from the joys and pains of the human condition. The former student of Aristotle opens a dialog, attempting to understand these people and their beliefs. He learns from them that man must experience an infinity of lifetimes, that existence is only a punishment, a way of atoning for previous mistakes. He listens to them for a long time and discovers with amazement the existence of "nirvana," the state that allows escape from the continuous chain of reincarnations in which man is perpetually wandering. Is Alexander the Great attracted by Brahman wisdom (the same wisdom that fascinates many people in its present Hindu form)? Does he sense that this religion, which he has encountered on the farthest edge of the known world, will cross time and civilizations and continue to fascinate people many centuries after his own earthly death? One thing is certain: 2,300 hundred years ago, long before the birth of Christ, Alexander the Great met and spoke with representatives of what would later become the Hindu faith.

ACHILLES

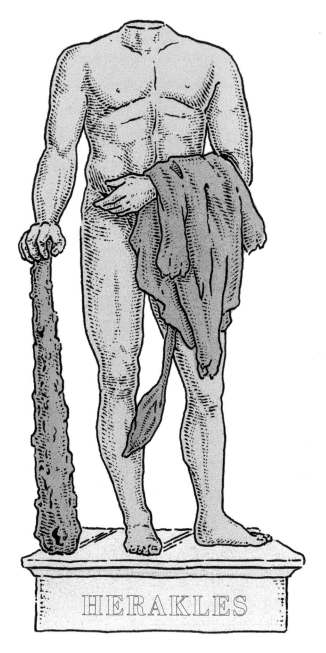

HERAKLES

Achilles and Odysseus are the most famous legendary heroes of Greek literature. Conqueror of Troy and slayer of Hector, the figure of Achilles thrills the youth of Alexander's time with his many exploits. So great is his renown that Alexander carries a copy of the Iliad with him wherever he goes. When the Macedonian lands at the Hellespont, he goes to visit the tomb of Homer's great hero and to honor Achilles' memory. Was Alexander the Great susceptible to his influence?

"On his father's side Alexander was a descendant of Herakles . . . from his ancestors on both sides he inherited the physical and moral qualities of greatness" (Diodorus Siculus, Universal History). A very popular hero among the Greeks, Herakles exerts a certain influence on Alexander the Great. At the very beginning of his eastern conquest, the Macedonian general orders the setting up of twelve columns ostensibly symbolizing the twelve heroic labors of the personage who later is known as Hercules by the Romans.

HE THINK HE IS?

DIONYSUS

Born in Macedonia, a region where the cult of
Dionysus is prominent, Alexander the Great is
initiated into this cult at a young age by his mother,
Olympias. It is no surprise therefore that Alexander
has great admiration for the god of wine and
unbridled pleasure. The most obvious sign of this
devotion is Alexander's constant participation—all
along the conquest trail—in many large and lively
Dionysian orgies.

PHARAOH

"When he reached Memp'..., hey sat him on the
sacred throne of Hephaestu . a ,d they dressed him in
a robe like an Egyptian king" (Pseudo-Callisthenes,
The Romance of Alexander the Great). Alexander as
an Egyptian pharaoh! After the difficult conquest of
Tyre at the end of 332, the king of Macedonia
annexes Egypt. Cleverly, the conqueror wins the
confidence of the Egyptian elite (and particularly the
priests) by consulting the oracle of Zeus-Ammon and
sacrificing to the local god.

1. Silver stater (Metapontum)
2. Gold diobol (Metapontum)
3. Silver decadrachm (Syracuse)
4. Silver tetradrachm (Danubian Celts)
5. Silver tetradrachm (Thrace)
6. Silver tetradrachm with the portrait of Alexander
7. Silver diobol (Delphi)
8. Silver stater (Thebes)
9. Silver stater (Corinth)
10. Silver tetradrachm (Athens)
11. Silver drachm (Elis and Olympia)
12. Silver tetradrachm (Barca)
13. Silver tetradrachm (Pergamon)
14. Silver tetradrachm
15. Electrum stater (Lampsacus)
16. Gold stater (Sardis)
17. Silver didrachm (Rhodes)
18. Electrum stater
19. Silver stater
20. Silver tetradrachm (Tyre)
21. Gold tetradrachm of the Ptolemies (Alexandria)
22. Silver tetradrachm of the Ptolemies (Alexandria)

THE GREEKS INVENT COINS

"For when they had come to supply themselves more from abroad by importing things in which they were deficient and exporting those of which they had surplus, the employment of money necessarily came to be devised" (Aristotle, *Politics*).

It seems that the idea of putting coins in circulation was born in a Lydian city (on the southern part of present-day Turkey) in the seventh century B.C. After that, the invention spread quickly through the Greek centers of Asia Minor and onto the Greek mainland. Depicting famous personages or things (kings, gods, symbols of cities), coins circulate from hand to hand and

are made from precious metals: gold, electrum (an alloy of silver and gold), and silver. Their purpose is to expedite payment in the political arena (financing public works in cities), the military (pay of mercenaries), and also to serve wider commercial needs. A medium that mirrors the fortunes of individuals and cities, coins bring about the appearance of a new class of people, bankers. Their role is to facilitate currency exchanges between cities, and the banker's position becomes gradually more important within the framework of economic life. It's worth noting that during the fourth century B.C. bankers are often freed slaves!

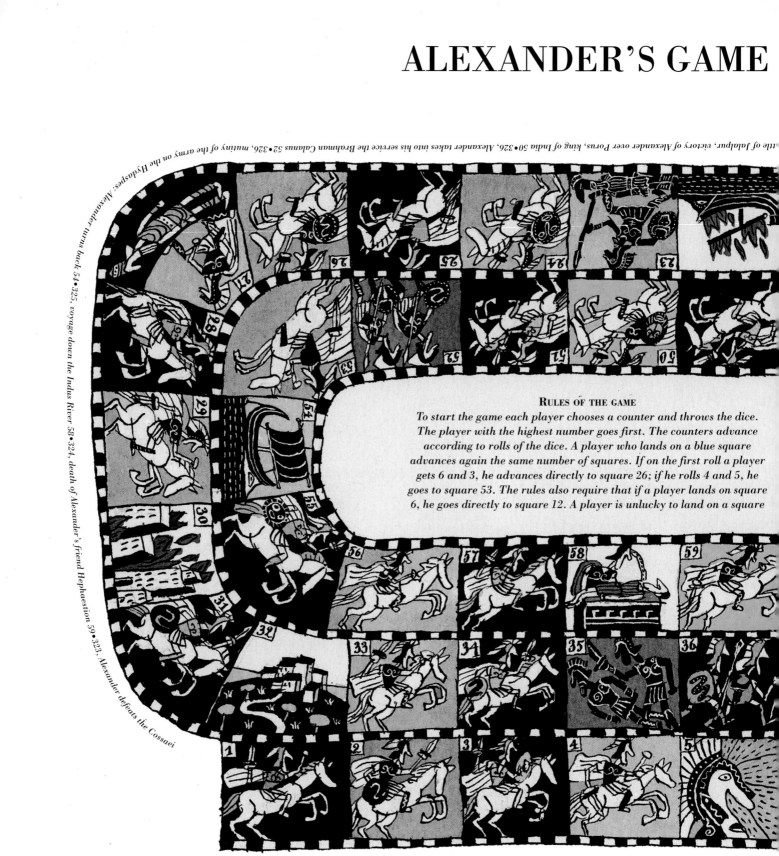

title of Jaīpur, victory of Alexander over Porus, king of India 50•326, Alexander takes into his service the Brahman Calanus 52•326, mutiny of the army on the Hydaspes; Alexander turns back 51•325, voyage down the Indus River 58•324, death of Alexander's friend Hephaestion 59•323, Alexander defeats the Cossaei

RULES OF THE GAME

To start the game each player chooses a counter and throws the dice. The player with the highest number goes first. The counters advance according to rolls of the dice. A player who lands on a blue square advances again the same number of squares. If on the first roll a player gets 6 and 3, he advances directly to square 26; if he rolls 4 and 5, he goes to square 53. The rules also require that if a player lands on square 6, he goes directly to square 12. A player is unlucky to land on a square

5•336, Alexander becomes king of Macedon 6•334, battle of the Granicus, victory over the Persians 9•333, the Gordian knot 14•333, battle of Iss

Great fans of entertainment, Alexander's contemporaries love games of all types. The Greek calendar is spread with religious and civic games and contests, whether gymnastic or literary competitions, foot or chariot races. In the fourth century B.C. such distractions are extremely varied, with special games for each age group. For the youngest there are games with small toys or rattles. Teenagers amuse themselves with balls, knucklebones, hopscotch, circles, tops, and even nuts that serve as a type of marbles. For adults there are dice and the much beloved board games (*petteia* or *kuboi*).

OF THE GOOSE

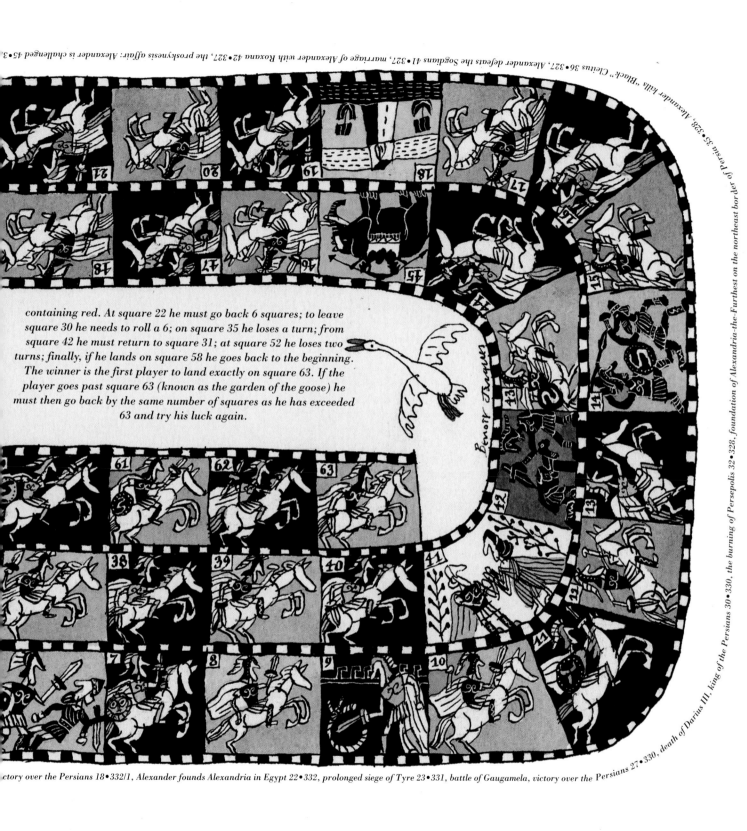

containing red. At square 22 he must go back 6 squares; to leave square 30 he needs to roll a 6; on square 35 he loses a turn; from square 42 he must return to square 31; at square 52 he loses two turns; finally, if he lands on square 58 he goes back to the beginning. The winner is the first player to land exactly on square 63. If the player goes past square 63 (known as the garden of the goose) he must then go back by the same number of squares as he has exceeded 63 and try his luck again.

These are more highly developed than Egyptian or Near Eastern games, part of the game is often a circular path, with each player trying to be the first to finish. Do Alexander's contemporaries really have the leisure time to play the goose game? There are plenty of reasons to think so. In fact, the concept of a game employing a path sprinkled with squares that either reward or punish is certainly a Greek invention. It appears again centuries later in the Florence of the Medici, in the form of the game of the goose, often used for teaching purposes.

IN ALEXANDER'S DAY AS OURS: DRINKING KILLS

"He drank and made merry with Medius; and then having arisen and bathed, went to sleep, and afterward dined with Medius, and again drank till late at night" (Arrian, *Anabasis of Alexander*).

A fervent follower of the cult of the god of wine Dionysus, Alexander the Great frequently goes to banquets. Between military maneuvers or while in winter quarters, the Macedonian enjoys even more of these parties, the consequences of which are sometimes quite serious. At Persepolis (in modern Iran) on April 25, 330, a huge drinking bout is organized, an event that leads to the destruction of a large part of the city, including the majestic royal palaces. During the winter of 327, at Bactra, the weddings of Alexander and numerous other Macedonians are abundantly supplied with wine. In 324, a drinking competition is organized at Susa and is won by a certain Promachus, who drinks 12 quarts of wine. No one is too surprised when the winner dies three days after his "glorious" victory.

In 330 B.C. the Greeks burn Persepolis, ceremonial capital of Persia

As the campaign goes on, the number of feasts organized by Alexander increases, and alcohol begins to take control of the conqueror's senses. He becomes less patient, is more easily angered and more unpredictable. On November 6, 328, a tragedy takes place: during another drinking party near Maracanda (present-day Uzbekistan), "Black" Cleitus, chief of the royal squadron and Alexander's foster brother, criticizes the king's conciliatory politics toward natives. Alexander is thoroughly drunk and loses control: "He leapt up and, as some say, snatched a spear from one of the guard and therewith smote and slew Cleitus" (Arrian, *Anabasis of Alexander*). Afterward, for three days the murderous king refuses to eat, wash, or shave for he has just killed one of his closest companions.

During the last six years of his life, physical and moral fatigue, setbacks, the increasingly open opposition of his army, and the death of his intimate friend Hephaestion push Alexander increasingly toward wine and drunkenness. As if ordered by the gods, it is at the end of a banquet in Babylon that the Macedonian catches the awful fever that will bring his death.

IN THE EAST, THE GREEKS TRY ON PERSIAN SKINS

Alexander the Great is a great champion of integration. Throughout his eastern conquest, between 334 and 323 B.C., the Macedonian tries his best to promote a bold policy of cultural fusion. If the elite classes of conquered countries submit to Alexander's ideals, they are allowed to preserve their position. From Scythia to Babylonia, the people governing some 30 satrapies (administrative regions of the ancient Persian Empire) are not chased from their positions. The same goes for representatives of the priestly class as well as those in charge of the military. In fact, every nobleman has the opportunity to preserve his former position if he will only join with Alexander.

What is the real reason behind this drive to integrate? In truth, Alexander the Great doesn't have much choice. Having come east toward new conquests with barely 10,000 men and not having the military manpower to fully pacify the conquered territories, the Macedonian is obliged to deal with the Persians. He continues to do so till the very end.

Persian or Greek? The empire conquered by Alexander the Great soon constitutes a mixture of elements from the two cultures. The Macedonian conqueror himself begins to be confused, virtually forgetting where he is: after having asked many of his men to marry Persian women, he requires them to treat him as if he were a Persian monarch! This problem comes to a head in the famous incident of the *proskynesis* (327): after adorning his head with the Persian tiara and surrounding himself with a guard that is the mirror image of the "Immortals" of Darius (the elite Persian guards), Alexander commands his men to perform in front of him the *proskynesis*, a ceremonial genuflection that the Persians offer to their sovereign. Many soldiers are outraged, and this paves the way for further conflicts between Alexander and his men.

The king's power has been threatened from within. Internal struggles like the plot of Philotas (330) and the mutiny of the cadets (327) are symptoms of the increasing uneasiness of the men. Blind or insensitive to these events, Alexander pursues his policy of integration with enthusiasm. During the winter of 326 B.C. he reorganizes the army: Persian contingents are incorporated into the Greek cavalry, a unit previously off-limit to outsiders. The Macedonian hoplites begin to murmur that Alexander is deliberately siding with the barbarians, thus dishonoring Macedonia and espousing the East. It's the last straw; during the summer of 326 the army refuses to pursue the conquest eastward. Ironically, by wanting to integrate, the conqueror brings an end to his dream of a universal empire.

YESTERDAY

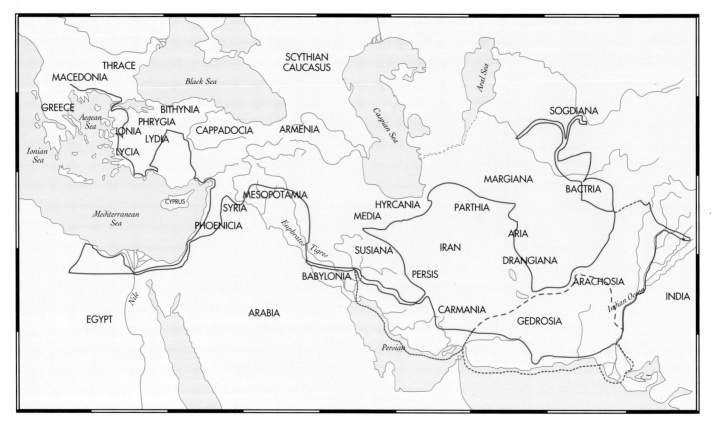

—————— *Route followed by Alexander the Great*

When they leave the kingdom of Macedonia in 334 B.C., Alexander the Great's soldiers cannot imagine that they will not see their families again for some twelve years and that first they will travel about 20,000 miles to reach the borders of the known world of that time—the *oikoumen*. The Hellespont, Thrace, Phrygia, Media, Hyrcania, Parthia, Bactria, Sogdiana: the regions the Greeks travel across seem faraway and strange even today.

The route followed by Alexander the Great is impressive when laid across a modern map. Leaving Greece, the Macedonian soldiers traverse in turn Turkey, Syria, Lebanon, Israel, Palestine, and Egypt. After a short stop in Egypt, they retrace their steps, but shifting northward to reach Jordan. Then, heading ever eastward, they pass through Syria again then Iraq, Iran, Afghanistan, Tadzhikistan, and Kirghizstan.

TODAY

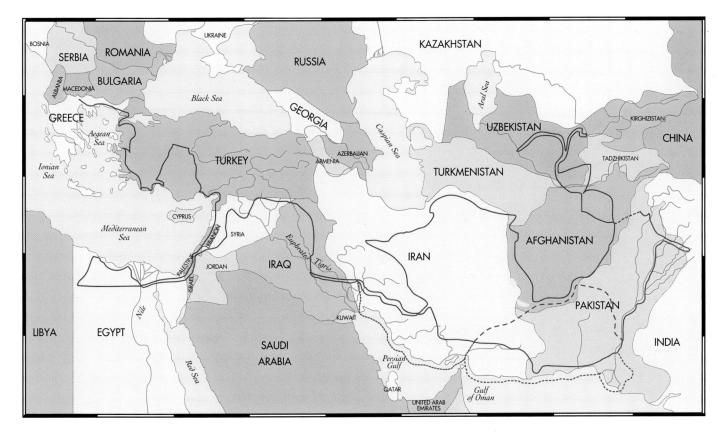

—————— *Route followed by Alexander the Great*

Europe is far behind them, as are the shores of the Mediterranean: the Greeks now thrive in the heart of Asia,

in a completely alien environment. Obsessed with the idea of universal conquest, Alexander heads on into India,

to the mountains of the Hindu Kush, before going down again through Pakistan. Between 334 and 323 B.C.

Alexander the Great and his armies traverse and conquer a total of some fifteen of today's countries—they annex

a new country almost every ten months. To do so, the army must defeat armies and rebellious peoples, found

cities, open roads, and bring along their administrative, political, and military knowledge.

This is a huge kingdom, its length from west to east close to 5,000 miles! With this in mind it is not surpris-

ing that both Julius Caesar and Napoleon looked upon Alexander the Great as the archetype of the military

conqueror. Even in the future, the Macedonian will serve as the shining example of conquest.

IF ONLY BUG SPRAY

"He drank and made merry . . . and slept where he was, the fever being already upon him" (Arrian, *Anabasis of Alexander*). The chronicler Arrian tells us in this sentence about the death of Alexander the Great in Babylon, on the evening of June 10, 323 B.C. The circumstances of his death are not clear. Did Alexander succumb after ten days of endless agony because he burned from "thirst and love," as the contemporary historian Paul Faure suggests? Or was he murdered by his cupbearer Iolus during a drinking bout? Or perhaps he was a victim of a physical ailment: a coma, a psychosomatic disease, or a massive depression developed after the death of his childhood love Hephaestion.

HAD BEEN INVENTED

Nearly all the biographers of the great Macedonian have offered his or her own hypothesis. The most probable seems to be that at age 32 Alexander contracted the dreaded disease malaria, which is transmitted by the bite of an infected mosquito. Fever, chills, devastating thirst—the symptoms related by the chroniclers (some of whom witnessed the Macedonian's agony firsthand) suggest this diagnosis. Alexander the Great, conqueror of the east, omnipotent king, finally laid low by an insect? It's hard to believe, but, as Sophocles wrote, "Bound, hand and foot, to fatal destiny . . . Alas! we living mortals, what are we but phantoms all or unsubstantial shades?" (*Ajax*).

DIODORUS SICULUS

Universal History

Died after 21 B.C.

"When he, at length, despaired of life, he took off his ring and handed it to Perdiccas. His friends asked, 'To whom do you leave the kingdom?' and he replied, 'To the strongest.' He added, and these were his last words, that all of his leading friends would stage a vast contest in honor of his funeral. This was how he died after a reign of twelve years and seven months."

QUINTUS CURTIUS (RUFUS)

History of Alexander

First Century A.D.

"Once when a messenger arrived, showing signs of a great joy in his expression, Alexander said, 'What are you going to announce to me which is worthy of such happiness, unless perhaps Homer has come to life?'"

ARRIAN

Anabasis of Alexander

Second Century A.D.

"He would not have remained content with any of his conquests, not even if he had added the British Isles to Europe; he would always have searched beyond for something unknown, and if there had been no other competition, he would have competed against himself."

PLUTARCH

Lives of the Noble Grecians and Romans

Second Century A.D.

"Alexander was but twenty years old when his father was murdered, and he succeeded to a kingdom beset on all sides with great dangers and rancorous enemies."

PSEUDO-CALLISTHENES

The Romance of Alexander the Great

Third Century A.D.

"For when he was weaned and developed in size and shape, he did not resemble in the least Philip and Olympias . . . but he developed features of a singular type. He had the hair of a lion and one eye was blue, the other dark. His teeth were as sharp as fangs. His physical appearance very clearly indicated what he would become."

GUSTAVE DROYSEN

Alexander the Great

Berlin: G. Finke, 1834

"However, Alexander just really escaped death, and even though his wounds had not yet closed, seven days later his life was no longer in danger. . . . A huge outcry came out from the chests of his veterans. They raised their hands toward the sky and tears of joy mixed with their cries of cheerfulness."

WRITTEN ABOUT ALEXANDER

ULRICH WILCKEN
Alexander the Great
Translated by G. C. Richards
New York: Norton, 1967

"By the humanity with which after battles he cared for the wounded, he won the hearts of his soldiers. To his Macedonian officers he preserved to the end the attitude of a comrade. Though not imposing in figure . . . he dominated everybody with his wonderfully bright eyes."

PETER BAMM
Alexander the Great: Power as Destiny
London: Thames and Hudson, 1968

"At the end of the exhausting day, Alexander was sitting beside a campfire on a small chair. . . he saw a veteran who had been with him at the Granicus totter towards the fire, half snowblind. The king rose and urged the old man to sit down on his chair. Having thawed out, the soldier suddenly recognized Alexander . . . He jumped up with a start, but Alexander merely smiled and said, 'If you had sat on the king of Persia's chair it would have meant death. Because it is Alexander's chair you are restored to life.'"

R. D. MILNS
Alexander the Great
London: Robert Hale, 1968

"It was from his conquests that Alexander obtained the glory he was striving after and there can be no doubt that he was a great conqueror. Indeed, he quickly became the type of the great conqueror and as such exerted considerable influence on that most militaristic of peoples, the Romans…Julius Caesar, it is said, when governor of Spain wept before a statue of Alexander at Cadiz because he had not accomplished at that age one fraction of what the Macedonian had achieved."

PETER GREEN
Alexander the Great
New York: Praeger Publishers, 1972

"The king may have demanded deification in his own lifetime, but he got mythification after he was dead. While his physical remains, hijacked by Ptolemy to Alexandria, lay on view in a glass coffin, his legend took root and flourished. By the time world-conquest came into fashion again, with Augustus, Alexander was already a giant, a demigod, a superhuman figure of romance."

MARY RENAULT
The Nature of Alexander
London: Allen Lane, 1975

"He had loved his fame. Like Achilles, he had traded length of days for it. He had trusted in the gods to keep their bargain; and, like Achilles, not in vain."

ROBIN LANE FOX
The Search for Alexander
New York: Little, Brown & Co.: 1980

"Pupil of Aristotle, he too came to a view through Greek eyes of the merit and nobility to be found among the best men of Asia. His plans for concord are awesome, unequaled before or since. But in his greatness, other features are perhaps more telling— the use of his father's solid power base, the grand ambition of youth and its new generation, the sense of a close relationship with the gods, and the driving impulse of the Homeric hero's epic ideal."

INSIDE US, WE ALL HAVE

With Alexander gone, the empire was left to the greed of his former military chiefs and was quickly divided. The fusion between East and West that Alexander had so ardently desired fell apart. The influence of the Greeks, however, did not weaken. For nearly three centuries, Hellenism—commercial, as well as political and cultural—continued to reign

Sempé

SOMETHING OF GREECE

over the territories conquered by Alexander's armies. The Greek model was apparent every-where: Greek was spoken in Alexandria, and Greek games were organized in Antioch (in today's Syria). In fact, the spirit of Greek civilization spread over the entire world, just as another great spirit continues to fascinate and enliven our culture today—Alexander the Great.

July 356—Birth of Alexander at Pella (Macedonia). His parents are King Philip II of Macedon and Queen Olympias.

337—Meeting at Corinth of all the Greek cities (except Sparta) and creation of the Corinthian League. Greece is unified.

Summer 336—Assassination of Philip II. Alexander (who is 20 years old) becomes Alexander III (the Great) and is recognized as king of Macedon.

Fall 336—Blitz campaign of Alexander in Thessaly. At the meeting of the Corinthian League, he obtains confirmation of his nomination as a chief general (*hegemon*) in the war against Persia.

Spring 334—Alexander leaves Macedonia naming Antipater as regent. The army arrives in Asia.

May 334—On the banks of the Granicus River, the Greeks are victorious against the Persians.

Spring 333—In Phrygia, the mythical episode of the Gordian knot takes place.

November 333—At Issus, the Greeks rout the forces of Darius III of Persia.

Up to the fall of 332—Alexander enters Phoenicia (the present Syro-Palestinian coast). The city of Tyre mounts a great resistance, its siege lasting nine months.

332—Siege of Gaza, which lasts two months. Alexander is wounded in the shoulder by an arrow.

Winter 332-spring 331—Alexander is in Egypt. He visits the oasis of Siwah, where he consults the oracle of the god Ammon, and founds the city of Alexandria.

October 1, 331—The third confrontation with the armies of Darius III takes place on the plain of Gaugamela. Once again, the Persians are driven to flight.

Winter 331-spring 330—At Persepolis, the armies of Alexander destroy the city. During the spring the royal palace will be entirely destroyed by a terrible fire.

Spring 330—Alexander reaches Ecbatana, ancient capital of Media. Alexander decides to set up the financial administration of his empire in this place.

Spring-summer 330—Murder of Darius III, king of the Persians.

Fall 330—Plot of Philotas against Alexander the Great. Philotas and his father, Parmenion, are executed.

329-328—Alexander reaches Sogdiana, the eastern region of the Persian Empire. A series of clashes takes place between the Greeks and the local populations.

328—Foundation of Alexandria-the-Furthest, on the northeast border of the former Persian Empire.

Fall 328—During a particularly drunken banquet, Alexander kills "Black" Cleitus, the commander of the royal squadron.

ALEXANDER'S REIGN

Spring 327—Alexander vanquishes the last resisting Sogdians.

327—At Bactra, Alexander marries Roxana, the daughter of a Bactrian nobleman.

327—The so-called cadet conspiracy; this time, the conspirators are royal pages. They will be stoned to death.

327—The incident of the *proskynesis* (prostration). Opposed to this Persian custom demanded by Alexander, some of the Greeks refuse to obey. A plot instigated by Callisthenes is discovered. The culprit is imprisoned then sentenced to death.

Spring 327-winter 326—Reorganization of the army: eastern soldiers are henceforth to be recruited; this measure meets with strong opposition from the Greeks.

Fall 327-326—The army crosses the Hindu Kush, and Alexander founds Alexandria-of-the-Caucasus. The army is divided in two.

Spring 326—In Taxila, among the Brahmans, Alexander gains the services of an Indian wise man, Calanus.

May 326—On the banks of the Hydaspes River, Alexander faces and vanquishes Porus, the sovereign of India.

Summer 326—Mutiny of the army: the Greek soldiers refuse to cross the Hydaspes River and to pursue further conquests to the East. Alexander is obliged to turn back.

November 326—Alexander orders the building of a fleet. He has the army embark on the ships and goes down the course of Hydaspes.

325—Continuation of the river trip onto the Indus River. The army makes many discoveries of local flora and fauna. Several times Alexander confronts the local populations.

September-October 325—The nightmare crossing of the Gedrosia desert: many women and children perish because of thirst and exhaustion.

Fall-winter 325—Alexander and a part of his troops reach Carmania (present-day Kirman), where they join up with Craterus and Nearchus' fleet.

March 324—In the royal palace of Susa, weddings of Alexander with Parysatis and Statira, the daughters of Artaxerxes III Ochos and Darius III respectively. Hephaestion, Alexander's right-hand man, also marries a daughter of Darius III, Drypetis.

July 324—Revolt of the Macedonian soldiers against Alexander, who wishes to discharge all veterans in the army. Thirteen soldiers will be executed, after which the Persian armies are integrated.

October 324—Death of Hephaestion, Alexander's friend. Alexander is overcome by immense grief.

Winter 324-323—Alexander conquers the Cossaei, the people of Luristan.

June 323—After a banquet and ten days of terrible suffering, Alexander the Great dies at Babylon, in the palace of Nebuchadnezzar.

INDEX

BOOKS FOR FURTHER READING

Arrian. *The Campaigns of Alexander*. Trans. by Aubrey de Selincourt. New York: Penguin, 1976.

Boardman, John; Griffin, Jasper; Murray, Oswyn. *The Oxford History of Greece and the Hellenistic World*. Oxford and New York: Oxford University Press, 1991.

Curtius, Quintus (Rufus). *History of Alexander*. Trans. by John Yardley. New York: Penguin, 1984.

Fox, Robin. *Alexander the Great*. New York: Penguin, 1994.

———. *The Search for Alexander the Great*. New York: Little, Brown, 1980.

Green, Peter. *Alexander the Great*. New York: Praeger, 1970.

Hamilton, Edith. *The Greek Way*. New York: W.W. Norton, 1993.

Nardo, Don. *Ancient Greece*. San Diego: Lucent Books, 1995.

Plutarch. *The Lives of the Noble Grecians and Romans*. Trans. by John Dryden, edited and revised by Hugh Arthur Clough. 2 vols. New York: Modern Library, 1992.

[Pseudo-Callisthenes]. *The Greek Alexander Romance*. Trans. by Richard Stoneman. New York: Penguin, 1991.

Tarn, W. W. *Alexander the Great*. Chicago: Ares, 1981.

Wilcken, Ulrich. *Alexander the Great*. Trans. by G. C. Richards. New York: Norton, 1967.

ILLUSTRATIONS

PHOTO CREDITS